Pearson's Canal Compa[nion]

STOURPORT RING

BLACK COUNTRY RING
Dudley & Stourbridge Canals

Published by J. M. Pearson & Son
Tatenhill Common, Burton-on-Trent, DE13 9RS
Telephone (0283) 713674

Third Edition 1992. ISBN 0 907864 59 7

Maps by Malcolm Barnes
Cartographer of Burton-on-Trent.

Typeset by Character Graphics
of Taunton, Somerset.

Printed by Penwell
of Callington, Cornwall.

Introduction

THE STOURPORT RING is an 83 mile, 118 lock circuit of canals and part of the River Severn located in the counties of Worcestershire and West Midlands. Its chief appeal lies in the contrasting character of the individual canals which go to make it and the variety of landscapes – both urban and rural – that it passes through. For an average boat crew it would take in the order of 7½ hours cruising time per day to complete in a week.

ANOTHER well known, though misleadingly named, circuit contained within this guide is the BLACK COUNTRY RING, which is nowhere near as industrial in character as the name implies. In common with the Stourport Ring it incorporates the Birmingham Canal Navigations main line between Wolverhampton and Birmingham, but otherwise belies its name, being located predominently in the county of Staffordshire, and passing through the delicious scenery of the upper Trent Valley, past the timeless canals junctions of Fazeley, Fradley and Great Haywood. At 74 miles and 79 locks it should take no longer than around 5½ hours cruising per day to do in a week.

ALTHOUGH the 'Stourport' and the 'Black Country' are the two most regularly cruised 'rings' covered by this guide, reference to the Route Planner will suggest several other circular routes which are possible. The most ambitious itinerary could take in the largest loop of all: Stourport – Great Haywood – Fradley – Birmingham – Worcester – Stourport; 127 miles and 149 locks with an average cruising time of 65 hours. A much more modest circuit could include Aldersley Junction – Dudley Port – Parkhead – Stourton – Aldersley; 34 miles, 71 locks, 22 hours. This 'mini-circuit' could be achieved in under 4 hours cruising per day if you devoted a week to it; a gentle and facinating exploration of the idyosyncratic charms of the real Black Country.

Tardebigge Locks, Worcester & Birmingham Canal

THE STOURPORT RING.

FOR ALL PRACTICAL purposes, Stourport is the head of navigation on the Severn, and it is here that the through traveller by water exchanges the fluctuating currents of the river for the stolid waters of the Staffordshire & Worcestershire Canal. Stourport itself suffers from a split personality, half convinced that it is a seaside town, half a rich heritage of canal wharves, vying with Shardlow on the Trent & Mersey in Derbyshire as the best preserved example of an early inland port. But whether you have come here for a ninety-nine and a knees-up, or to pay more serious homage to Brindley's basins, Stourport does not disappoint. To moor in the Upper Basin hearing time being measured by the quarter beats of the Clocktower's sonorous bell is one of the inland waterways most magical experiences. And whatever entrance the boater makes – locking up from the Severn under the benign gaze of the Tontine Hotel, or descending into the dripping depths of York Street lock from the canal – there will be few steerers who will resist exploration of the remaining basins, shunting back and forth like some busy tug, turning in wide arcs or honing their locking skills.

Remaining basins? Yes, there are four now, the original and largest – now known as the Upper Basin – opened in 1771, and connects through two wide-beam 'barge' locks with the river. These impressive (at least in narrowboater's eyes) chambers were built sturdily enough to withstand the Severn's perennial propensity for flooding, and capacious enough for the indigenous Severn Trows. Between the barge locks lies the

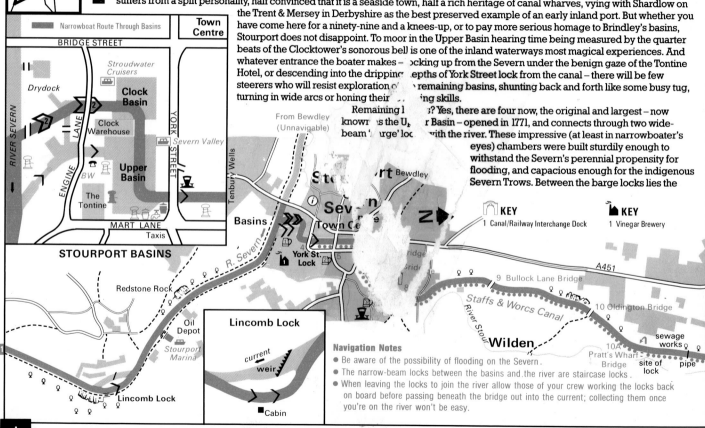

Town Centre

STOURPORT BASINS

Narrowboat Route Through Basins

BRIDGE STREET

Stroudwater Cruisers

Drydock

Clock Basin

Clock Warehouse

RIVER SEVERN

LANE

Upper Basin

BW

The Tontine

ENGINE

YORK STREET

Severn Valley

MART LANE

Taxis

From Bewdley (Unnavigable)

Tenbury Wells

Stourport

Severn

Bewdley

Town Centre

Basins

York St. Lock

KEY
1 Canal/Railway Interchange Dock

KEY
1 Vinegar Brewery

A451

9 Bullock Lane Bridge

10 Oldington Bridge

Staffs & Worcs Canal

River Stour

Wilden

Redstone Rock

Oil Depot

Stourport Marina

Lincomb Lock

sewage works

10A
Pratt's Wharf Bridge

site of lock

pipe

Lincomb Lock

current

weir

■ Cabin

Navigation Notes
- Be aware of the possibility of flooding on the Severn.
- The narrow-beam locks between the basins and the river are staircase locks.
- When leaving the locks to join the river allow those of your crew working the locks back on board before passing beneath the bridge out into the current; collecting them once you're on the river won't be easy.

21

smallest surviving basin, thought to have been used as an assembly point and not as a wharf as such. A second link to the river, consisting of four narrow-beam locks in pairs of staircases, was opened in 1781. Here again the locks are separated by a small basin from which a drydock extends. At the top of the narrow locks, and contemporary with their construction, lies the Clock Basin, inter-connected with the Upper Basin. On a peninsular between these upper, boat-filled expanses of water stands the glorious Clock Warehouse, headquarters now of the Stourport Yacht Club whose comparatively huge vessels migrate up the river to winter in the security of the basins.

Two more basins dating from the early 19th century lay to the east of Mart Lane. The lower, reached through a wide lock, had only a brief existence, closing in 1866 when the gas works took over the site. But the other basin flourished for an 'injury time' of commercial activity between 1926 and '49 when coal boats for the power station discharged in it, their dusty black cargoes of slack being unloaded by electric grab and carried in hoppers along an aerial ropeway to the power station furnaces.

The River

The Severn's present official head of navigation is approximately ¾ mile upstream of Stourport Bridge at the point where the Gladder Brook enters from the west bank, though David Hutchings, the midlands architect who led the Stratford-on-Avon Canal and Upper Avon restoration schemes, has proposed bringing back navigation to the Upper Severn, a relatively easy objective were it not for the distrust of riparian landowners. One waterway project which did not materialise was for a canal from Stourport to Leominster. A token sod was dug opposite the basins in 1797, but the

ludicrously ambitious through route never came to fruition.

Lincomb Lock is currently, then, the highest on the Severn. It lies in a picturesque setting dominated by one of the sheer red sandstone cliffs which characterise the river in this part of the world. There is another such dramatic outcrop between Lincomb and Stourport known as Redstone Rock, according to a contemporary Bishop of Worcester, a refuge of outlaws, in Cromwell's time. Opposite this an oil depot and a well piled wharf mark the destination of the Severn's last commercial traffic above Worcester, an activity which ceased in the Sixties. Nearby the River Stour enters the Severn unobtrusively from behind some blocks of concrete.

The Canal

Exiting unobtrusively from Stourport, like someone trying to creep away from a party, the Staffs & Worcs Canal makes its way through unkempt meadows bordering the Stour. It seems as quiet as the proverbial grave hereabouts and the towpath tends to be overabundantly vegetated in summer. Between bridges 7 and 8 an un-numbered span marks the course of the Hartlebury and Bewdley branch line, the original route of the Severn Valley Railway. There used to be a canal/rail interchange dock at this point; mooring rings set into the high brick retaining wall recall these busier times, and on the towpath side you might spot a roller around which a line would be taken to aid manoeuvring into the tight-angled loading dock. Another echo of by gone trading days is encountered by bridge 10A, through which a branch canal long ago led down through a lock into the River Stour, by which route boats reached Wilden Ironworks across the valley.

KIDDERMINSTER comes and Kidderminster goes, briefly putting paid to the Staffs & Worcs inclination for self-communion. South of the town two isolated locks, couched in the shadow of sandstone outcrops, are separated by a high viaduct over which the steam trains of the Severn Valley Railway puff and pant their way between Kidderminster and Bridgnorth, a worthwhile excursion if you have time to spare. In any case, 'Kiddey' creates its own austere beauty: the high chimneys of the carpet mills looming over the cut, and the towpath switchbacking over side bridges spanning abandoned arms like a Mexican Wave. The town's best moorings lie above the lock overlooked by the imposing parish church. To the north the canal quickly establishes its more obvious charms, delving into glades of balsam and convolvulus, bluebells and foxgloves; an aquatic nature trail spared the intrusive formality of interpretive paraphernalia.

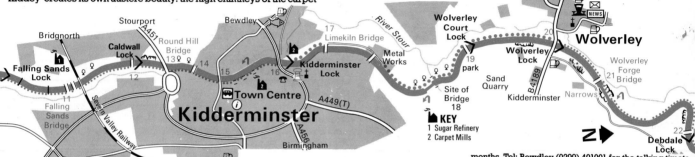

Eating & Drinking

LITTLE TUMBLING SAILORS (1) – Mill Lane, west of bridge 16. Delightfully eccentric Little Pub Co. house with a nautical theme and a suitable emphasis on seafood. Children catered for.

KING & CASTLE (2) – Comberton Hill. Instant nostalgia in the SVR's refreshment room. Guest beers and home made food.

Shopping

The shopping centre is lively and traffic free and there's a retail market on Thursdays and Saturdays.

Places to Visit

SEVERN VALLEY RAILWAY – One of Britain's premier preserved railways, the SVR runs up the valley to the Shropshire market town of Bridgnorth, a delightful ride in its own right, never mind the attraction of steam. Services run from March to November, daily in the summer months. Tel: Bewdley (0299) 401001 for the talking timetable; 403816 for other details. TOURIST INFORMATION CENTRE for Kidderminster and Wyre forest district located at the SVR station. Tel: Kidderminster (0562) 829400.

Public Transport

BUSES – Midland Red West services throughout the area. Tel: 0345 212 555.

TRAINS – frequent local services to/from Birmingham, Stourbridge and Worcester. Tel: 021-200 2700.

Kidderminster

Somehow "come and see my new Kidderminster" doesn't have quite the same ring about it as "my new Axminster", but the tradition of carpet making goes back a long way in ths town, and although one of the canalside works was an early victim of the recession, the trade still occupies a good proportion of the workforce. A busy ring road divorces the canal from the town centre, but in the pedestrianised streets the roar of traffic soon dies down and there is a definite, though difficult to define, appeal to Kidderminster; not least its affinity for remembering its famous sons in statue form, or the sudden unexpected glimpses you catch of the pewtery waters of the Stour burrowing beneath its streets.

Wolverley

A charming village snuggled in folds in the sandstone hills. John Baskerville, the printing type designer, was born here in 1706. One or two houses back on to the sandstone and incorporate rooms hewn out of the rock. The centre of the village is about 10 minutes walk from bridge 20, canalside, however, is THE LOCK, a cosy Banks's 'Pint & Platter' pub with a good children's playground on the towpath side.

The section between Cookley and Gothersley finds the Staffordshire & Worcestershire Canal at its unimpeachable loveliest. There is a 'Toytown' ambience to this canal which the Swiss would heartily approve of. Perhaps the prettiest length of all lies between Hyde Lock and Dunsley's diminutive tunnel as, bordered by woods on one side, the waterway glides past meadows framed by a conifer plantation. It would be difficult to dream of a more pastoral scene, and yet a huge ironworks stood here for two centuries. In the heyday of the works twenty puddling furnaces produced wrought iron and the buildings lined the canal for some distance. Only the

Kinver

Village Centre

Kinver Lock

Dunsley

Hyde Lock

Course of Kinver Light Railway

Bridgnorth

Waterworks

Devil's Den

Stourton Castle

Stour Aqueduct

Stourton Junction

Stour pond

Wolverhampton

KEY
1 Pumping Station (Site of Light Railway Terminal)
2 Hyde Ironworks
3 Cookley Iron Works

Cookley

Cookley Tunnel 65 yards

pumping station

Worcs

Caunsall

Austcliff

Staffs

River Stour

Whittington Lock

Dunsley Tunnel 25 yards

A449

Stewponey

A458

Stourbridge Canal

Stourbridge

iron-master's house remains, demurely dwelling on its past on the towpath side above the pretty lock. One is awestruck that such an undertaking can vanish so completely. But then comes realisation that the same process of change and renewal is taking place throughout the neighbouring Black Country, as the traditional heavy industries of the region are replaced with urban forests and shopping malls.

Barely had the ironwork's pandemonium ceased when a new interloper arrived on the Stour Valley scene in the shape of a curious little narrow

gauge railway operated with electric trams. The Kinver Light Railway opened in 1901 and lasted only 29 years, but brought thousands of day-trippers from the Black Country to Kinver, advertised by the operating company as 'the Switzerland of the Midlands'. On Whit Monday, 1905, 16,699 passengers were carried along the 5 mile line from the "Fish Inn", Amblecote. The 3ft 6ins gauge being compatible with the Black Country's main tramway network, saw through cars running to Kinver from as far away as Birmingham. The line crossed the canal at Stewponey and ran parallel with it to the terminus at Mill Lane, Kinver.

Stewponey was a focal point of boat traffic on the Staffs & Worcs, and here could be found a wharf, stables, toll office, workshop and employees cottages. British Waterways use the yard now as a maintenance base. Even after the Second World War, in excess of fifty boat loads of Cannock Chase and Baggeridge Colliery coal per week were being worked through

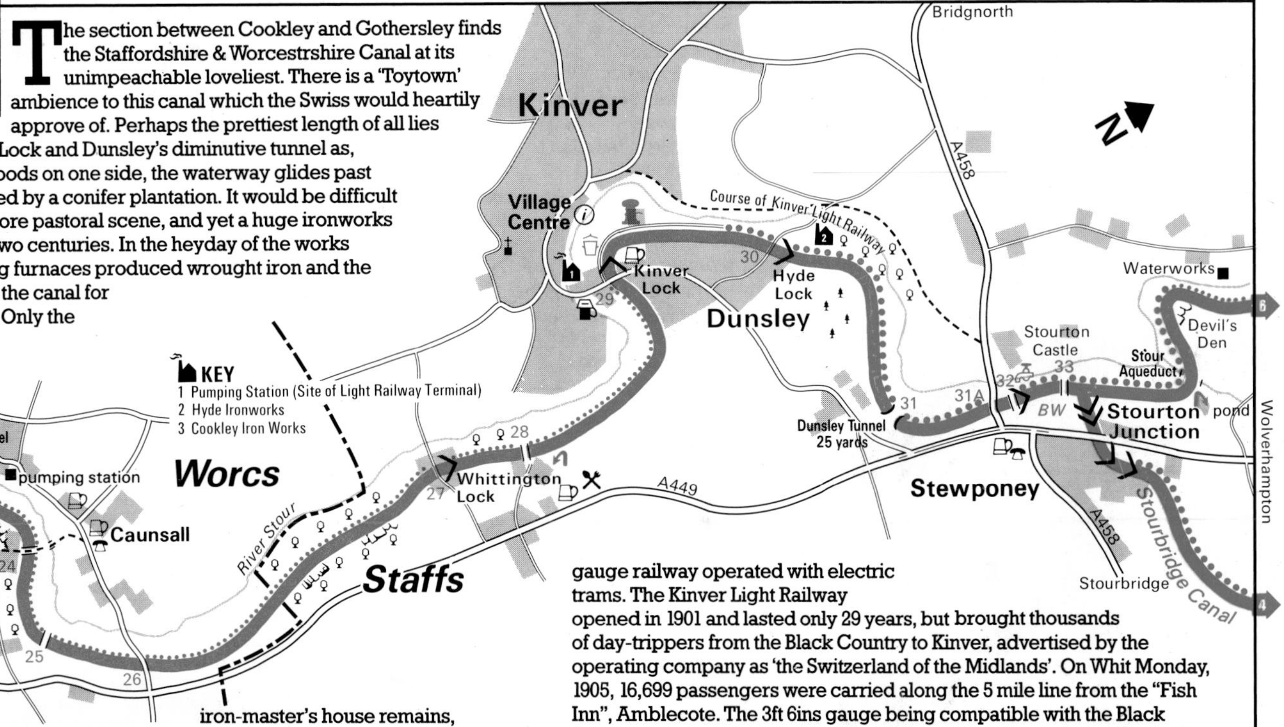

Stewponey on their way down to Stourport power station. But in 1949 the National Coal Board announced a florin surcharge on each ton of coal loaded on to boats and, not entirely surprisingly, the traffic was transferred to rail. Someone in high places obviously had a vested interest in bringing about such a change. A few years desultory trading of day boats to Swindon steel works, 'railway' boats off the Stourbridge Canal, and occasional cargoes of baled wool to Stourport from 'up north' followed, and then, without anyone really noticing, the working boats were gone.

Stewponey doesn't find its way on to the Ordnance Survey maps, but it is a name of local currency, thought to be derived from an old soldier, returning with a Spanish wife from the town of Estepona, who opened an inn here, the name of which was soon corrupted by Black Country vowels. The inn became a road house in the Thirties, one of these huge joints which people drove out to in the early days of motoring when there was still an element of romance to be found on the roads; there was even a 'lido' in the grounds at one time.

At STOURTON JUNCTION four chambers raise the Stourbridge Canal 43 feet on its way up into the Black Country. As we've written elsewhere, canal

junctions do not come much more attractive than this and, even if your itinerary commits you to the Staffs & Worcs, you could do worse than spend the night in Stourbridge, little more than an hour and a half away: turn to Map 4!

North of Stourton Junction the Staffs & Worcs performs an S bend to bridge the River Stour. The setting is idyllic, the river tumbling over a shallow weir just upstream of the aqueduct. Close by, a peculiar cave is cut out of the rocks at water level. Known as the 'Devil's Den', it is thought to have been used as a boathouse by the Foley family of Prestwood Hall.

From this point on, southwards, the River Stour is the canal's constant companion, the man made waterway keeping pace with the river's gradual descent to the Severn by way of occasional, isolated locks of great charm. It is difficult to think of another canal bordered by so many trees, broken only by sudden outcrops of Triassic rock. The most dramatic of these – a real cliffhanger! – is near Caunsall where the Bunter pebble beds of Austcliff Rock loom over a bend in the canal. Little less spectacular is the canal's burrowing beneath COOKLEY, precariously overlooked by the houses on main street.

Cookley

A village with an iron-making tradition going back three centuries. There are two pubs and a fish & chip shop. A post office stores (open daily, EC Wed & Sun) butcher, small supermarket a shoe repairers make Cookley a useful and friendly port of call for the day's provisions.

Kinver

Kinver is well aware of its charms and flaunts them to the full. Visitors pour in during the summer months, filling car-parks at the rear of the pubs, restaurants and cafes which provide most of the fabric of the High Street. But somehow Kinver preserves its appeal and, especially in less frenzied seasons than summer, repays the 10 minute walk from the canal. In any case, the village's main asset is its superb setting in the shadow of Kinver Edge, a dramatic wooded ridge rising to 500 feet and the southern end of the 'Staffordshire Way' long distance footpath. For those with both time and energy at their disposal, the climb to the top of the Edge can be recommended. On a clear day you can see – well almost, as the song says, forever – certainly over to Bredon Hill and the Cotswolds. Also up here are the remains of rock houses, some incredibly used as dwellings until halfway through this century.

Eating & Drinking

VINE INN – canalside bridge 29. M&B beer, bar food, nice waterside garden.

COOKLEY IRONWORKS

PLOUGH & HARROW – High Street. Unprepossessing 'local' worth patronising for the medal winning Batham's ales.

Many other pubs, cafes and restaurants in the village centre. Fish & chips too.

Shopping

All the shops (and there is a good choice for such an otherwise small village) congregate along the main street. Galleries and gift shops abound and there is a good secondhand bookshop if you need to stock up on your holiday reading matter. Barclays have a branch bank in the centre. If you are in too much of a hurry to stop long, the garage near the canal sells fast food and provisions.

Things to Do

Local tourist information – such as leaflets describing the local walks – is available from Traveller's Joy in the High Street (Tel: Dudley (0384) 872940).

Public Transport

BUSES – successor to the light railway, but not half as romantic, there is an hourly bus link with Stourbridge. Tel: 021-200 2700.

DUDLEY & STOURBRIDGE CANALS.

THE CANAL COMPANIONS, it is widely known, have a tendency to wax lyrical; in these pages, at least, the spirit of romance remains alive and kicking. So when we tell you that the pound between Stourton and Wordsley junctions is simply *ravishing*, the more cynical and world weary amongst you will take it with a pinch of salt. Frankly, though, there is a precarious beauty about the Stourbridge Canal as it winds past Primrose Hill and through woodland above the Stour, which, in our experience, is only equalled by the Caldon Canal in the Churnet Valley. There are much prettier, more vivacious canals, to be sure, but their settings are guaranteed and obvious; here it is the sheer unexpectedness of the Stourbridge Canal's charm which bowls you over.

A modest aqueduct over the Stour preceeds WORDSLEY JUNCTION and the opportunity for a detour up the Town Arm to the excellent moorings at Stourbridge Wharf. The arm terminates at the foot of Stourbridge High Street (though it once proceeded a short distance beyond to a railway transhipment wharf) beside a restored bonded warehouse with an upper storey supported by cast iron columns. Secure moorings (access to and from which is via a locked gate which only opens to those with a BW sanitary station key) and a friendly lady caretaker, make this a thoroughly pleasant spot for an overnight stay.

The STOURBRIDGE SIXTEEN raise or lower the canal to the tune of 148 feet between the junctions at Wordsley and Leys. Back in the 1950s these locks were derelict and it took much work and lobbying by enthusiasts to bring about a U turn in British Waterways corporate apathy to the decay of the Stourbridge Canal. Despite being in a predominantly built-up area, the flight is an enormously attractive one, especially as it passes the glassworks between locks 12 and 13, with its huge firing kiln, or cone, reminiscent of a Potteries landscape. Alongside the chamber of lock 12 stands a timber warehouse, whilst locks 9 and 10 are telescoped together like a mini-Bratch. Overlooking the adjoining side pond is 'The Dock', a general store and off licence with a tradition of serving boatmen past and present.

At LEYS JUNCTION the feeder channel comes in from Fens Pools and it is possible to navigate the short distance up to the junction of the erstwhile Stourbridge Extension Canal at Brockmoor if, that is, you are not averse to a little pushing and prodding with your barge poles. Between Leys and The Delph the Stourbridge Canal forms a defensive moat between two generations of housing: the austere post war council estates of Brettell Lane

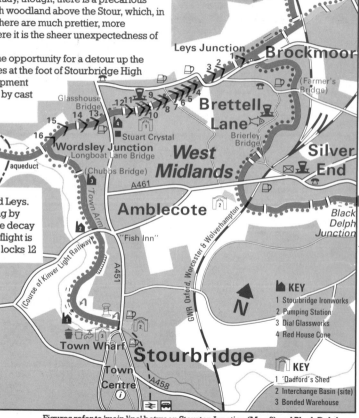

KEY
1 Stourbridge Ironworks
2 Pumping Station
3 Dial Glassworks
4 Red House Cone

KEY
1 'Dadford's Shed'
2 Interchange Basin (site)
3 Bonded Warehouse

Figures refer to 'main line' between Stourton Junction (Map 3) and Black Delph Junction: allow half an hour in each direction for the Stourbridge Town Arm.

on one side, the festoon curtained mews of the upwardly mobile on the other. All the canal traveller can do is subconsciously arbitrate. Passing under the old Oxford, Worcester & Wolverhampton Railway, the view opens out briefly across the Amblecote Valley to Stourbridge. Time and time again comes the disquieting thought that, in terms of distance, you haven't travelled very far at all; but in experience of the profit and loss of life, the gap is immeasurable. Two side bridges, formerly serving the Delph Iron Works, herald BLACK DELPH JUNCTION and the head-on meeting with the Dudley No.1 Canal.

Stourbridge

From the canal wharf, it is but a short walk through the underpass beneath the ring-road – which encircles the glass-making town of Stourbridge like a boa constrictor – to the town centre. And how unexpected, for Stourbridge is not yet another Black Country industrial community, but rather a market town with a profusion of shops and some not uninteresting architecture. Even the usually restrained Pevsner was moved to label the former grammar school (on your left as you ascend the High Street) 'picturesque', whilst a little further on stands the town clock; imposing, fluted-columned, cast in the local iron works in 1857, and equipped with a match-striking plate (a typical piece of Victorian thoughtfulness and ingenuity) for passers by.

Eating & Drinking

Adjacent to the canal wharf is a Chinese takeaway and the MOORINGS TAVERN, a free house frequented by local boaters where bar meals and snacks are usually available. There is no children's room as such, but there is a canalside patio in use during the summer months. Opposite the clock in Coventry Street the FRENCH CONNECTION bistro and adjoining delicatessen look appealing. Banks's have a PINT & PLATER SKITTLE CLUB not far from the basin on the ring-road. The ROYAL EXCHANGE on Enville Street is a CAMRA recommended Batham's house. Alongside lock 5 on the Stourbridge flight THE SAMSON & LION is an enterprising free house offering a choice of local brews and a range of meals and snacks as well as morning coffees and afternoon teas during the summer.

Shopping

Stourbridge has a daily market, whilst two precincts play host to all the major chain stores. MR BUMBLES delicatessen on Market Street continues to flourish, the staff – the female members anyway – wear spotless frilly aprons, and there is a mouthwatering selection of meats and regional cheeses on sale. Several of the local glassworks have factory shops.

Things to Do

TOURIST INFORMATION – The Library, Stourbridge. Tel: Dudley (0384) 394004.
FELLOWS, MORTON & CLAYTON – boat trips along the Stourbridge Canal from the town wharf. Tel: Dudley (0384) 375912.
STUART CRYSTAL – Red House Glassworks, adjacent lock 12 of the Stourbridge flight. Factory tours, museum and shop. Tel: Dudley (0384) 71161.

Public Transport

BUSES – Centro services throughout the area. Tel: 021-200 2700.
TRAINS – frequent shuttle service on BR's shortest branchline to Stourbridge Junction station for connections to/from Birmingham, Kidderminster and Worcester. Tel: 021-200 2700.

"THE DOCK"

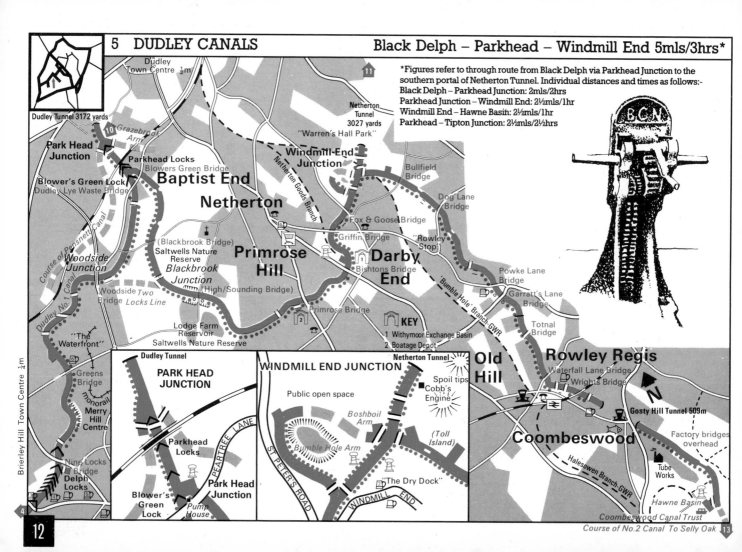

THOUGH AMALGAMATED with the BCN as long ago as 1846, there is about the Dudley Canals an independence of style and spirit marking them apart from the bulk of the system on the other side of the Rowley Hills. Mid 19th century improvements – by-passing some of the more circuitous loops; construction of Netherton Tunnel; substitution of the original nine locks at The Delph by eight new ones – left their legacy of BCN characteristics. But, emerging from the gloom of Netherton's south portal, or crossing the invisible junction at the foot of Delph Locks, you can almost grasp the change in atmosphere; a new variation on an old theme.

The Dudley Canal Line No.1 – to give it its official title – runs for just 4½ miles between the junctions at Black Delph and Tipton. But in this brief distance the No.1 packs a great deal of fun for the present day canal traveller. There are two lock flights, an extraordinary tunnel, and numerous scene changes as the canal traverses the urban and industrial landscapes of four centuries.

DELPH LOCKS are marked miles ahead by the high-rise blocks of Brierley Hill. This is one of the most dramatic and photogenic flights in the country. Since 1858 there have been eight chambers with a total rise and fall of 85 feet. Six of them are laid tightly together like an acquatic escalator, and the adjoining weirs cascade spectacularly if there is a surplus of water in the cut. The top and bottom chambers occupy their original sites, but when first opened in 1779 there were *seven* other locks running in a still discernable course to the east.

Having become familiar with the 19th century environs of The Delph, the next bend in the canal opens out to reveal a glimpse of things to come, the 21st century vista of the Merry Hill Centre, one of the new era of out of town shopping developments akin to Meadowhall near Sheffield or the Metro Centre at Gateshead. Monorail trains snake along elevated tracks like something out of a science fiction film, and the temples of consumerland glisten and ripple in the brittle Black Country sunlight. Beyond Greens Bridge the canal eases its way through The Waterfront, a billion pound development, mixing commerce with leisure, and occupying the site of the once vast Round Oak steel works. Arguably the most satisfying building of the development is the pub, a stylised cross between an East Anglian water mill and a Black Country foundry with plenty of mock weatherboarding and reconditioned brick; now there must be a moral in that somewhere.

Passing the former junction of the Two Locks Line at Woodside Junction, the canal reaches Blowers Green Lock and PARKHEAD JUNCTION, sandwiched between a cement silo and a pumping house. Many years have passed since Parkhead was truly a junction, but 1992 marked the re-opening of DUDLEY TUNNEL to through navigation. Details relating to operation of the tunnel were vague as we went to press. British Waterways advised that the tunnel's ban on powered craft will be upheld, and that it is likely that through craft will be hauled by tug. We recommend you check with BW or your hire base if you plan to include the tunnel in your itinerary. The opportunity to pass through the tunnel, and to see some of its caverns and basins en route, certainly fires the imagination.

The Dudley No.2 Canal once totalled 11 route miles and linked the Dudley No.1 Canal at Parkhead with the Worcester & Birmingham Canal at Selly Oak (see Map 13). It was completed in 1798 and included Britain's fourth longest tunnel at Lapal (3795 yards), a daunting, towpath-less bore subject to a unique system of operation. A steam pumping engine produced an artifical bi-directional current through the tunnel to aid the momentum of boats passing through. But the tunnel was prone to subsidence and closed during the Great War.

Between Parkhead and Windmill End junctions the Dudley No.2 Canal clings to the 453ft contour, essaying a broad loop around the resonantly named communities of Baptist End, Netherton and Primrose Hill. Occasionally the factories recede to reveal the distant wooded tops of the Clent Hills rising to a thousand feet southwards beyond Halesowen. BLACKBROOK JUNCTION retains its roving bridge, spanning the course of the ill-fated Two Locks Line, built to by-pass Parkhead in 1858. But like much else in this honeycombed region, it suffered from subsidence, and was abandoned as beyond repair in 1909.

There is so much to see on this section, and so little room to mention the highlights here, that you should really be referring to our "BCN Canal Companion", which has more 'elbow room' in which to describe the fascinating remnants of the past which make travel along this canal so rewarding. By Bishtons Bridge a development of industrial premises occupies the site of Netherton Ironworks where the anchors for the *Titanic* were cast. There was a great tradition of chain and anchor making in this particular corner of the Black Country, a peculiar anomaly in an area so far removed from the sea. Apparently much of the chain making was done by women packed tightly in small premises which became so hot that they habitually worked bare-breasted. Would that the Black Country had had an artist of the calibre of Joseph Wright of Derby to do justice to such scenes. The nebulous workshops on the new estates seem mind-numbing in comparison.

The old rail/canal exchange basin at Withymoor has been adopted for private moorings by a local trust, but they also offer temporary accommodation for passing boats. Good informal moorings are to be had at WINDMILL END JUNCTION, perhaps the epitome of the Black Country canal scene, with its profusion of Toll End Works roving bridges, basins and arms; and overlooking all this, the haunting image of Cobb's Engine House, as if somehow transmuted from a Cornish cliff top.

From Windmill End, scene of the 1991 National Rally, the main canal route now leads through NETHERTON TUNNEL to the BCN main line at Dudley Port. You might enjoy, however, an excursion down what is left of the Dudley No.2 line as far as Hawne Basin. Long after Lapal Tunnel was closed in 1917 this route remained in commercial use to serve the tube works at Coombs

Wood on the far side of GOSTY HILL TUNNEL. Indeed, a degree of trade existed until 1974, though after this the canal would certainly have deteriorated but for the emergence of the Coombeswood Canal Trust, whose secure moorings at Hawne, on the outskirts of Halesowen, flourish as a centre for the Black Country's private boaters. The highlight of a voyage down the arm is the passage through Gosty Hill Tunnel, 557 yards long and as snug as a piston in a cylinder. At the far end of the tunnel the canal emerges into the murky catacomb of the tube works, widening as water lilies thrive where Joey boats thronged.

Brierley Hill

Once everyone found employment in the steelworks, but now prosperity lies in the lap of Merry Hill, claimed to be Britain's largest out of town retail, commercial and leisure complex. The Richardson twins, whose brainchild this is, want to put it even more firmly on the map by building the world's tallest tower here; at 2022ft, twice as high as the Eiffel Tower.

Eating & Drinking

Brierley Hill bristles with pubs, and in Delph Road boaters who number beer amongst their co-enthusiasms, will find that they have hit a rich seam. HPD's THE BELL (3) and Banks's THE TENTH LOCK (4) stand either side of the bottom lock of the Delph flight, the former typical of its owners nostalgic style, the later new and smart and confusingly named (it *would* have been a good joke if they had counted the *present* number of locks first!). Eastwards up the road there are Hansons and Courage houses, but the froth on the pint is THE VINE (5) – better known as the Bull & Bladder – Batham's brewery tap, and one of the really great Black Country hostelries. In complete contrast (though ironically doing its best to imitate a Victorian pub) is Banks's BREWER'S WHARF (6) by Green's Bridge, a not entirely unlikeable all day pub serving a wide range of food. Just a monorail ride away, are the myriad fast food outlets of the Merry Hill Centre: PIZZA HUT, McDONALDS and many others, notably DRUCKERS VIENNA PATISSERIE for gourmets of West Midlands gateaux.

Shopping

Brierley Hill High Street stubbornly goes about its 19th century retailing tradition while Merry Hill draws in the

Black Delph.

crowds, sucking trade from all over the West Midlands; and rent free for 10 years too, much to the chagrin of Dudley, Wolverhampton and Birmingham. "All your favourite shops and stores," boasts the brochure; over 200 of them with attendant banks and building societies to make sure you come with cash and credit to spray about with gay abandon. Access from the canal is easy from Green's Bridge, but they still haven't provided any mooring rings or steps down from the steep embankment: third rate facilities for those third rate enough in outlook to come by canal. Also of possible interest is the proximity of the UCI MULTISCREEN cinema to the canal here. Tel: (0384) 78282.

Netherton

The black tower of the parish church of St Andrews crowns a bald, windswept summit. Cholera victims of the early 19th century are buried in unmarked common graves in the churchyard, from the back of which there are vistas to be had over the canal and Saltwells Nature Reserve. The little town itself shelters in the lee of the

hill, but was noticeably less bustling than on previous research trips.

Eating & Drinking

Netherton built its reputation on coal and iron, but nowadays it's the pilgrimage to the OLD SWAN/MA PARDOE'S (1) which brings strangers here. It is one of the best known Black Country pubs because they still brew on the premises, and so popular had it become that the original bar, with its enamelled ceiling swan and solid fuel stove, spilled over into the adjoining building where a more lounge-like atmosphere prevails, and where substantial home-cooked meals are available. Meanwhile over at Windmill End, stands the celebrated DRY DOCK (2), one of the Little Pub Company's endearing outlets where the theme is canals, as conveyed by the provision of a bar in the shape of a narrowboat. As usual you are urged to drink 'harder and faster', and if you can wipe the dish clean containing one of their Desparate Dan Cow Pies you can claim a glutton certificate.

Shopping

The shops are looking a little sorry for themselves now, so patronise them while you can. Morale boosting cakes from Firkins.

Public Transport

BUSES – frequent service to/from Dudley. Tel: 021-200 2700.

Coombeswood

Useful pocket of facilities (shops, pub, fish & chips) above the southern portal of Gosty Hill Tunnel. Access official now!

THE COUNTRYSIDE EMPTIES. Wales is only the width of an OS map away. These are the landscapes of Francis Brett-Young, a writer yet to be rediscovered by the mass paperback publishers, though still easily found on the shelves of second-hand bookshops. No-one has ever written better about the area between the Black Country and the Welsh Marches. You should try "Far Forest" or "Dr Bradley Remembers"; either would make admirable reading material before 'light's out' on your cruise.

Smestow Brook, a tributary of the Stour, is now the canal's chief confidant and friend. In the woods below GOTHERSLEY LOCK stand the ruins of a canal company roundhouse, a twin to the one at Gailey on the Watling Street, now restored and used as a canalside shop. Both roundhouses date from the year of Trafalgar, and this one at Gothersley marks the site of an important canal wharf provided to serve a sizeable ironworks which existed on this site until the 1880s. Staggering, isn't it, to think of all the vanished activity; and how the forges and furnaces, tramways and wharves of a century ago have been superseded by ivy and ash, balsam and butterbur: time passes its fingertips across the face of the years in a fleeting caress of fortune and failure.

GREENSFORGE is a delightful mooring place. Its name recalls the existence of another vanished forge, one which became a mill, the big, four-square building of which remains intact and glimpsed through the alders and willows which line the Smestow. Stroll down the lane and you'll discover its macey, long dry mill pond, an obvious declivity in the reed beds. Nearby an arm extends into Ashwood Basin, now a marina but once

an important interchange basin with the Kingswinford Railway, a colliery line dating from 1829 whose first locomotive, *Agenoria* is now in the National Railway Museum's collection in York.

Between Greensforge and Hinksford locks the canal is bordered by the contrasting images of woodland and a huge static caravan park. Hinksford pumping station is one of several waterworks in this part of the valley. Yet another ironworks lined the canal at SWINDON, though this one survived until as recently as the early 1970s; not that you would credit it now, the site being covered, not by flora and fauna, but by the neat lawns, potting sheds and garden gnomes of a housing estate. The works was owned at one time by the Baldwin family, of which Stanley became a prime minister. Note how the towpath briefly changes sides so that it did not run through the works' precincts. BOTTERHAM LOCKS are a staircase pair, so remember to ensure that the top chamber is full and the bottom empty to start with. They raise or lower the canal over twenty feet. North of here the canal becomes temporaily embroiled with the industrial fringe of Wombourn.

Summary of Facilities

The NAVIGATION INN, canalside by bridge 37 at Greensforge, is an comfortable Davenports pub, justly popular with boaters despite the apparent decline in taste of Davenports beer since closure of the brewery in Birmingham and transfer of production to Nottingham. Bar meals are usually available and there is a nice canalside garden. There are four pubs at Swindon, one near bridge 38, the others best approached from bridge 40. Our favourite is THE GREEN MAN near Swindon Lock, a tiny Banks's house which somehow contrives to do food as well. A stone's throw west of bridge 40 there's a fish & chip/doner kebab shop together with a useful row of shops (post office, general store and newsagent) the only shopping handy to the canal between Kinver and Compton.

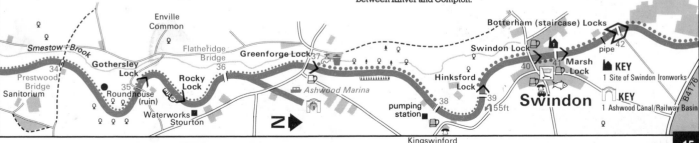

THE BRATCH is notorious in canal circles, for here the boater is confronted with a flight of three unique locks, squeezed so closely together that one takes them for a staircase, and consequently sets about operating them in quite the wrong way. Faced with a sudden descent in the valley of the Smestow, Brindley *did* originally provide a staircase of three chambers here, but at the expense of predictable water wastage and traffic delays, and a remedy was soon sought. Ingeniously, the flight was rebuilt as separate locks with intervening pounds extended sideways through culverts.

At the foot of The Bratch is a picnic site in the grounds of a pumping station opened in 1896. The architect held scant rein to his Gothic flights of fancy and the result would not look amiss in any remake of "The Prisoner of Zenda". Two steam engines pumped water from deep boreholes in the Bunter Sandstone rocks below until being replaced in 1960 by more efficient but less engaging gas turbines. Until their demise coal was brought in by canal to feed the furnaces. The presence of such sandstone in the rock strata beneath the Smestow and Stour valleys led to a profusion of such pumping stations along the course of the canal.

Above Bratch the countryside is open and rolling and there are glimpses westwards of the Clee Hills, marred only by pylons marching grotesquely

across the landscape to Penn Grid Substation. The towpath evaporates in the vicinity of Dimmingsdale Reservoir (provided for the canal but seldom called upon now) and through walkers are faced with an uncomfortable detour past set-faced fishermen. Better, perhaps, to take to the railway walk running parallel to the east.

Below Bratch the canal skirts Wombourn, skirmishing with industry. The red scars of former sand quarries abound. Narrowboats carried sand from numerous wharves hereabouts up to the Black Country forges for mould making in the casting process. The fragmented nature of the landscape seems to rub off on its inhabitants. Gardens are often untidy, derelict cars decompose in spinneys, and cast-out furniture rots in haphazard bundles – a prime example, sociologists will tell you, of environmental influence. West of bridge 44 Giggety Lane fords the Smestow Brook.

Eating & Drinking

WAGGON & HORSES – canalside bridge 43. Hansons, bar lunches Mon-Fri, garden with play area.

ROUND OAK – canalside bridge 45. M&B, bar meals, garden, families catered for. Nice etched windows.

Navigation Note

BRATCH LOCKS should be operated exactly as ordinary locks, but because of the minuscule intervening pounds it is not possible to pass oncoming boats once they have begun to come up or down the flight. Remember to keep the top gate and paddles of each chamber closed as you are letting water out of the chamber above, otherwise a flood may result. Bratch can be a bottleneck at busy times, though the resident lock-keeper – based in the octagonal office (freshly restored to its brick faced origins) by bridge 48 – is usually on hand to oversee things. Do as he asks and prepare to be patient.

Wombourne Bridge 43

Bumble Hole Lock

ford

44 Giggetty Bridge

45 Houndel Bridge

46

47 48

picnic site Waterworks

Lock-keeper Bratch Locks 30ft.

Wombourn

public footpath & bridleway GWR·Wombourn Branch

49 Awbridge Lock

Electric Sub Station

Ebstree Lock

reservoir

52 Dimmingsdale Lock & Wharf

53

reservoir

54 Mops Farm Bridge

Castle Croft Bridge 55

Staffordshire

WOLVERHAMPTON'S WESTERN SUBURBS are what estate agents would term 'residentially desirable' and they harbour little hint of Black Country industry. Moreover the Staffs & Worcs closets itself away from the most pressing overtures of urbanisation, masquerading its way through wooded cuttings to and from a conspirator's assignation with the Birmingham Canal at Aldersley Junction.

If it's Thursday or Saturday afternoon, make time to stop at WIGHTWICK and visit the nearby manor, no feudal home of a local squire, but a late Victorian mansion which has been in National Trust hands for about 50 years. If you were of the opinion that Victorian architecture was stuffy and overbearing, this lovely house, dating from 1887, will revise your preconceptions. The interiors are furnished by William Morris and the walls are hung with Pre-Raphaelite paintings. The grounds are gorgeous too and there is a working pottery and bookshop.

Evidence suggests that COMPTON LOCK was James Brindley's very first essay in narrow lock construction. It was rebuilt in 1986 and it is interesting to note that the top gate came from Bradley Workshops on the BCN whilst the bottom pair were provided by British Waterways' depot at Northwhich in Cheshire. The chamber is graced by one of the Staffordshire & Worcestershire Canal Society's charming wooden name posts. The lock also boats one of the distinctive circular weirs peculiar to this canal.

An impressive girder bridge carries the trackbed of the Wombourn branch railway (not built until 1925, now a bridleway) over the canal on the outskirts of Tettenhall. Another interesting crossing sees bridge 62 take Telford's Holyhead Road. In this age of specialisation and anonymity, one can only marvel at one man's contribution to so many aspects of civil and industrial engineering. In the early years of the 19th century

communications between London and Dublin were appalling (politically, one is tempted to reflect, nothing has changed). Over twenty quite autonomous turnpike trusts were responsible for the road from London, via Shrewsbury to Holyhead, the port for Ireland. Yet, despite vociferous protests from travellers and the frequent failure of the Mail Coach to penetrate the wilds of Wales at all, matters were not brought to a head until the Act of Union between Britain and Ireland required the regular presence of Irish Members of Parliament at Westminster! Thomas Telford was invited to survey the route and plan improvements, which he did with characteristic thoroughness, recommending widening, resurfacing and numerous gradient modifications, as at the cutting through Tettenhall Rock. Telford's new road was opened throughout with the completion of his famous bridge over the Menai Straits to Anglesey in 1826.

Summary of General Facilities

COMPTON is a useful port of call for canal travellers before heading off southwards down the isolated course of the Staffs & Worcs. There is a good row of suburban shops reached within a minute of bridge 59. There are Oriental and Occidental take-aways and a Banks's 'Milestone' pub/restaurant. Frequent buses head for Wolverhampton. Calor gas and emergency boat repairs are handled by the LIMEKILN boatyard (Tel: Wolves (0902) 751147. Other suburban facilities are available at NEWBRIDGE by bridge 61.

Boating Facilities

DOUBLE PENNANT – Tel: Wolverhampton (0902) 752771. Calor gas, repairs & servicing, boatbuilding & brokerage, chandlery.
WOLVERHAMPTON PASSENGER BOAT SERVICES – Tel: Wolves 757494.

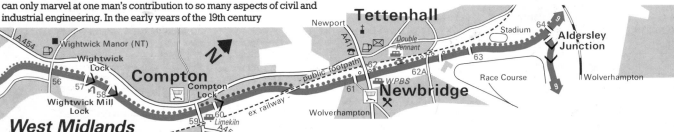

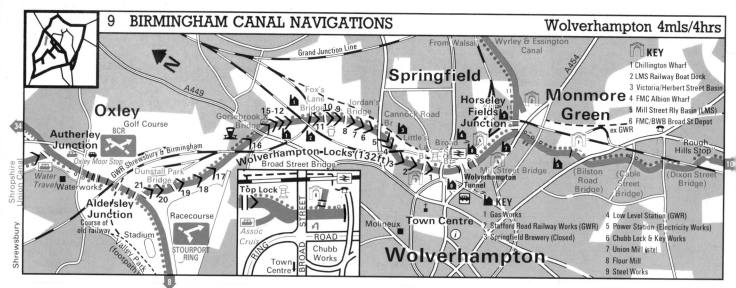

KEY
1 Chillington Wharf
2 LMS Railway Boat Dock
3 Victoria/Herbert Street Basin
4 FMC Albion Wharf
5 Mill Street Rly Basin (LMS)
6 FMC/BWB Broad St Depot

KEY
1 Gas Works
2 Stafford Road Railway Works (GWR)
3 Springfield Brewery (Closed)
4 Low Level Station (GWR)
5 Power Station (Electricity Works)
6 Chubb Lock & Key Works
7 Union Mill (site)
8 Flour Mill
9 Steel Works

BRINDLEY'S Birmingham Canal of 1772 encounters the proud and ancient manufacturing town of Wolverhampton. North of the town centre the canal negotiates a memorable flight of locks known, colloquially as 'The Twenty-one'. At its foot lies an unexpectedly rural junction with the Staffordshire & Worcestershire Canal at ALDERSLEY. In contrast, southwards from Wolverhampton, the main line of the BCN is accompanied by the crumbling legacy of the Black Country's industrial heritage. From HORSELEY FIELDS JUNCTION the Wyrley & Essington Canal wanders off eastwards to Walsall and beyond; as covered by our BCN Companion.

Rarely does a town seem to rub off on its canal as much as Wolverhampton does. Whoever landscaped the top lock got it just right. Picnic tables and flower beds could easily have resulted in municipal overkill. but there is a plausibility here which enhances the canalscape, compelling boaters to moor and make an expedition into this vibrant town which has ambitions of becoming a city. The present Broad Street bridge replaces an earlier structure that had cast-iron balustrades and ornate gas lamps which now resides in the Black Country Museum. The adjoining

warehouse was owned by Fellows, Morton & Clayton, the famous canal carriers, and stabling was provided for boat horses which were used to haul unpowered boats up or down the locks. Apparently the boat children were in the habit of riding these animals bareback, at breakneck speed down to Aldersley to collect upcoming boats. Another form of aid on the flight came in the form of 'hobblers', men or boys who would help single-handed captains through the locks for a suitable fee. Beyond the warehouse, and its arm spanned by a typical iron side bridge, the canal passes through a brick-lined cutting into a short tunnel, formerly the resort of Wolverhampton's ladies of the night.

The 'Twenty-one' is well maintained and somehow seems less exhausting than one might expect with so many locks to contend with in just a mile and a half of canal. Brindley only provided *twenty* chambers, but the last was so deep that it caused water shortages. In 1784 the bottom lock was reduced in depth and a short cutting excavated to carry the canal to a new lock built in the intervening pound. This extra lock – No.20 – gives its identity away by having only one bottom gate. Almost uniquely – one can only think of Aintree on the Leeds & Liverpool Canal in comparison –

Wolverhampton race course adjoins the lower part of the flight.

Wolverhampton has always been an interesting railway centre, and the once rival lines of the Great Western and London, Midland & Scottish railways span the canal at several points, notably on a pair of fine viaducts. Lock 11 must have been a trainspotter's idea of heaven when the best of Swindon and Crewe puffed imperiously overhead. Oxley Viaduct, between locks 16 and 17, marked the northern frontier of Brunel's broad gauge empire. Another relic of railway days is the large corrugated iron clad warehouse (now a builders merchants) by lock 2 which was built on the site of Victoria basin, one of the canal/railway interchange wharves that were a significant feature of the BCN network. The emerging railways quickly grasped that development of short haul traffic, to and from the numerous works firmly established beside the densely knit canals, was in their best interest. One, of what amounted to over forty, railway owned basins remains in surprisingly good condition at Monmore Green on the southern outskirts of Wolverhampton, and if you're boating it is worth mooring up by Bilston Road bridge and peering over the wall down on to the covered arm framed by rusty railway tracks, which seem to have fallen out of use since the previous edition of this guide.

South of Wolverhampton the BCN's main line pursues a winding course through a largely industrial area, but there is barely a dull moment as each bend in the canal intrudes upon a fresh variation on the Black Country theme of 'metal bashing'. At 'Rough Hills Stop' the canal narrows at the site of a former toll house, the pretty canalside cottage providing rare domestic interest in amongst all the workshops and factories.

Wolverhampton

Disembarking at the commendable moorings above the top lock, visitors to Wolverhampton might well be pleasantly surprised by the size and scope of a town which, in common with other proud Black Country boroughs, has a tendency to languish in shadows cast by Big Brother Birmingham. Wulfrunians will rapidly put you right. After all, their pedigree is more impressive than that of the upstart down the A41. Ethelred the Unready granted the town a charter in 985 – Birmingham had to wait two more centuries before being so recognised. In medieval times Wolverhampton was something of a wool centre, a way of life recalled by street names like Farmers Fold and Woolpack Alley. But the discovery of coal and iron turned Wolverhampton into a manufacturing town famous for lock making (notably by Chubbs, whose huge triangular works overlooks the canal, albeit now in use as enterprise units) metal toys, hardware and belt buckles. Today, like everywhere else, Wolverhampton has had to re-gear for the microchip age, though steel is still processed in the peripheries of heavy industry which still cloak the town. The status of a town may soon change too, for the Queen has been approached to confer the title of a city on Wolverhampton in 1992. It would be no more than the place deserves, and then if 'Bully' and the boys can get 'The Wanderers' back in the premier league the future will be rosy indeed!

Eating & Drinking

You don't expect Wolverhampton to be a culinary centre –

The "21"

and it isn't. Nevertheless there are plenty of down-to-earth town centre pubs capable of slaking the thirst of boat crews. Two personal favourites are: THE POSADA, a dark little drinking den opposite the Art Gallery serving Holts Entire and lunches Mon-Sat; and the GREAT WESTERN by the old Low Level station (turn right off Broad Street immediately beyond the railway and it's about 200 yards ahead) which does Holdens and Bathams and lunches Mon-Sat, decorating the bars with lots of evocative old photos of the station in its prime, but the word is that the pub is threatened by redevelopment, so go soon!

Shopping

The Mander and Wulfrun centres are modern precincts emblazoning all the inevitable names in plastic facia. But down sidestreets and up alleyways plenty of characterful local shops are waiting to be discovered by the discerning shopper. Try the faggots at any butcher, they are a Black Country delicacy; really! But perhaps the most distinctive shop of all is Snapes, the tea & coffee merchants, on Queen Street. After a visit to this establishment you'll never be able to look a cup of Typhoo or Maxwell House in the face again. There's a useful grocery section to the shop at Water Travel's boatyard at Autherley if you haven't the time or misplaced inclination to visit the town centre. Also handy for hurriers is the corner shop by lock 16.

Places to Visit

TOURIST INFORMATION CENTRE – 18 Queen Square. Tel: Wolverhampton (0902) 312051.

Public Transport

BUSES & TRAINS – respective stations directly adjacent to canal, access via Broad Street bridge. Local enquiries on 021-200 2700. Intercity services on: 021 643 2711

Boating Facilities

ASSOCIATED CRUISERS – Little's Lane, Wolverhampton (0902) 23673. 2 to 6 berth hire craft. Pumpout and other usual facilities.
OXLEY MOOR STOP – adjacent bridge 65 Staffs & Worcs Canal. Tel: (0902) 789522. Pumpout, diesel, gas, boatbuilding, repairs, trip boat, gifts and provisions.
WATER TRAVEL – Oxley Moor Road (Autherley Junction). (0902) 782371. 2 to 8 berth hire craft (Hoseasons). Pumpout, diesel, petrol, gas, slipway, lift-out & storage, boatbuilding & brokerage, repairs & servicing, short-term moorings, shop, payphone and toilets.

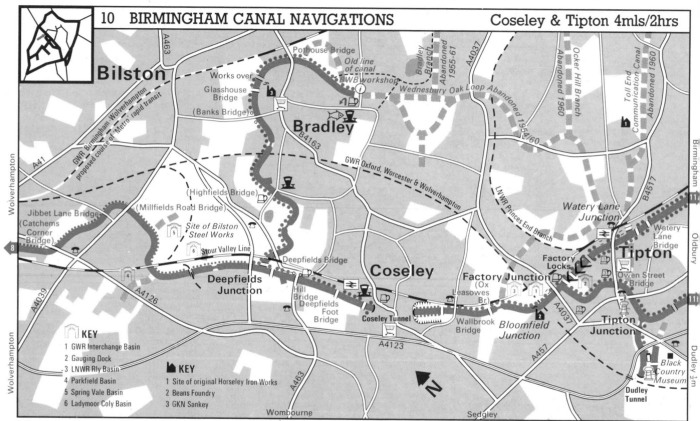

Bilston

Pothouse Bridge

Old line of canal BWB workshop

Works over

Glasshouse Bridge

(Banks Bridge)

Bradley

B4163

Bradley Branch

Abandoned 1955-61

Wednesbury Oak Loop Abandoned 1955/60

Abandoned 1960

Ocker Hill Branch

Abandoned 1960

Toll End Communication Canal

Abandoned 1960

GWR Birmingham-Wolverhampton proposed course of 'Metro' rapid transit

GWR Oxford, Worcester & Wolverhampton

A4037

Birmingham

A463

A41

Wolverhampton

(Highfields Bridge)

(Millfields Road Bridge)

Jibbet Lane Bridge (Catchems Corner Bridge)

Site of Bilston Steel Works

Stour Valley Line

LNWR Princes End Branch

Watery Lane Junction

Watery Lane Bridge

B4517

Oldbury

Tipton

Factory Locks

Owen Street Bridge

Deepfields Junction

Coseley

Factory Junction (Ox Leasowes Br)

Hill Bridge

Deepfields Foot Bridge

Deepfields Bridge

Coseley Tunnel

Wallbrook Bridge

Bloomfield Junction

Tipton Junction

A4126

A4039

A4037

A457

A4123

Dudley 1m

Black Country Museum

Dudley Tunnel

Wombourne

Sedgley

KEY
1 GWR Interchange Basin
2 Gauging Dock
3 LNWR Rly Basin
4 Parkfield Basin
5 Spring Vale Basin
6 Ladymoor Coly Basin

KEY
1 Site of original Horseley Iron Works
2 Beans Foundry
3 GKN Sankey

IN THE LATE EIGHTIES a very real sense of renaissance hung over the Black Country in general and the BCN in particular. Reclamation and refurbishment were eradicating decades of industrial decay and the canals were in the forefront of the Black Country Development Corporation's ambitious plans to revitalise the region. By coincidence, more boats were beginning to use these hitherto esoteric waterways, and altogether the future looked as bright as a well burnished tiller arm. But then the West Midlands came under the cloud of recession – once again – and the momentum of the previous few years was lost. Returning to these canals to research this edition, we found many of the proposed development schemes moribund, and canalside land reclamation spiralling into reverse. The section between Wallbrook and Ox Leasowes bridges, south east of Coseley, is a case in point. In 1988 the periphery of the towpath was a wasteland grazed by semi-wild ponies. A year later it was reclaimed and landscaped, pleasantly enough in a bland sort of way. But since then the weeds have taken over again, and though the ponies aren't back yet, they will need to be soon, if only to keep the grass down.

A glance at the accompanying map shows just how much of the BCN system was lost in the Fifties and Sixties. Trade was evaporating from the canals and the authorities hadn't the wit or imagination then to see the potential of retaining the waterways for leisure. Around a third of the Birmingham Canal Navigations total extent of 160 miles was abandoned during this Philistine period. The devotee, however, can trace much of it still, and in doing so daydream of boating itineraries impossible to recapture; a walk beside the remnants of the Bradley Branch is described in our "BCN Canal Companion".

Between Wolverhampton and Tipton the main line, in sinuous accord with the contours, betrays its largely Brindley origins. Only on the cut through Coseley – engineered by Telford in 1837 to by-pass the circuitous Wednesbury Oak Loop – do 19th century improvements take you away from the original route of 1772. At DEEPFIELDS part of the old loop is still navigable, a slender channel encroached by floating weed which leads to the Bradley workshops and offices of British Waterways. The south-eastern approaches to COSELEY TUNNEL are arboreous, the north-western, suburban. It is 360 yards long and contains a towpath on either side, that to the east being the most used.

Utilitarian nomenclature abounds of the BCN, and at FACTORY JUNCTION Brindley's *Wolverhampton Level* and Telford's *Birmingham Level* are seen to meet or divide, depending on your direction of travel. Heading for Birmingham you have a choice (always assuming both routes are free of stoppages!) between the directness of Telford's wide, embanked, twin-towpathed 'Island Line', 20ft below through the three

Factory Locks, and Brindley's original route which parallels it, hugging the 473ft contour in the shadow of the Rowley Hills. The latter affords water (but not towpath) access to the Black Country Museum where secure overnight moorings are available in the surreal environs of an 19th century time warp. Beyond the museum moorings is the northern portal of DUDLEY TUNNEL, first dug in 1775 to gain access to subterranean limestone workings. Ten years later it was extended through to join up with the Dudley Canal at PARKHEAD (refer to Map 5). Though closed to powered craft for many years, electric trip boats have carried passengers into the tunnel to see its spectacular caverns and open air basins, and now it is scheduled to re-open to through traffic again in 1992. Check with BW or your hire base for the latest position.

Two items of waterway history stand inconspicuously beside the top lock of the 'Factory Three'. On the towpath side one of the brick buildings adjoining the canal was used as a Boatmen's Mission, one of five such establishments on the BCN dispensing hot drinks, tobacco, washing facilities and a little transitory warmth and companionship. On the Sabbath the emphasis became more overtly religious and Sunday School was held for the boat children. Opposite, directly alongside the lock chamber, stands a building once used as a gauging dock, where BCN craft could be weighed to ascertain loading capacity, and thereby the appropriate rate of toll. FACTORY LOCKS have been landscaped and they create an attractive group, especially at the foot of the bottom lock where a little cast iron bridge all but spans the chamber to facilitate access to and from each side of the lock. East of here, Telford's route strides purposefully, in company with the electrified railway, towards the 'Second City', passing the site of WATERY LANE JUNCTION where the deliciously named Toll End Communication Canal cut across the main line on its way down from the *Wolverhampton Level* to join the Walsall Canal. BCN backwoodsman, 'Caggy' Stevens, resides in the old dock formed by the closure of the branch beyond the railway embankment.

Tipton

Tipton, once islanded by canals, was known locally as the 'Venice of the Midlands' long before the cliche regarding "Birmingham having more canals than Venice" became common currency. And even with the relegation of the Tipton Green & Toll End Communication Canal to a landscaped pathway, Owen Street – the main thoroughfare – remains embraced by the old and new main lines. Appropriately the town's most famous son, William Perry the

celebrated 'Tipton Slasher', England's champion prizefighter for seven undefeated years from 1850, began his working life as a canal boatman; an ideal occupation for the pugilistically minded. Tipton also has a modern day sporting hero in the shape of Steve Bull, the Wolverhampton Wanderers and England centre-forward.

Eating & Drinking

NOAH'S ARK (1) is a single-roomed Banks's pub decorated with photographs of old canal scenes; a place for drinking and talking and not eating. Food, on the other hand, comes heaped high on your plate at THE PIE FACTORY (2), one of the Little Pub Company's mind-boggling creations where food is just about the only thing they do take seriously. Back in the realms of conventionality you might try THE FOUNTAIN (3), a Holt, Plant & Deakin house which was once 'The Slasher's' headquarters. PERRY'S CAFE (Owen Street) also pays homage to the

Continued on page 24

CANAL BUSTERS are spoilt for choice as the old and new main lines of the Birmingham Canal Navigations pursue their respective, and intrinsically distinct courses between Tipton and Smethwick. Twice the routes are interconnected (three times if you are towpath travelling), creating a series of mini-rings within rings, tempting you to go round and round and round in ever decreasing circles.

Old Main Line

Brindley's route tends to be less boated than Telford's. Duckweed encroaches on the channel and moorhens and coots are confident enough in being undisturbed to build precarious nests midstream. East of TIPTON JUNCTION the *Wolverhampton Level* runs through council housing, passes beneath the old South Staffordshire railway, then finds itself in the much changed environment of 'Black Country Quays', a series of housing

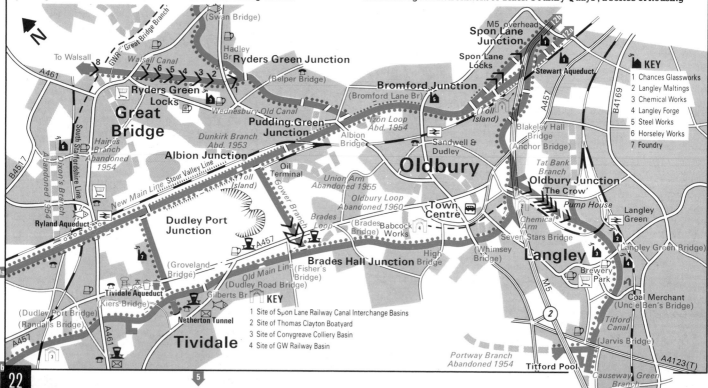

KEY
1 Chances Glassworks
2 Langley Maltings
3 Chemical Works
4 Langley Forge
5 Steel Works
6 Horseley Works
7 Foundry

KEY
1 Site of Spon Lane Railway Canal Interchange Basins
2 Site of Thomas Clayton Boatyard
3 Site of Conygreave Colliery Basin
4 Site of GW Railway Basin

developments gradually colonising the sites of former industry. One of them incorporates a large canal basin, emphasising the important role that the BCN is playing in the regeneration and 'greening' of the new Black Country.

TIVIDALE AQUEDUCT carries the old main line over the Netherton Tunnel Branch. There is no waterway connection here, but a path links the two levels, and if you have no immediate plans to journey through the tunnel (on foot, preferably with a torch, or by boat) then it is worth a short walk along the lower level towpath to see the tunnel's northern portal.

Meanwhile, back on Brindley's level, the next focus of attention for eastbound travellers is BRADES HALL JUNCTION where the Gower Branch descends through the BCN's solitary 'staircase' lock to join Telford's main line, half a mile to the north. Richardsons, the famous Black Country developers, run by twin brothers, have their offices here. Merry Hill (Map 5) is probably their best known scheme to date, they have also acquired the old Fort Dunlop tyre factory (Map 23) for which there is a plan for conversion into a luxury hotel.

More new waterside housing preceeds Babcock's large engineering plant, as the approaches Oldbury. There are views south towards the Rowley Hills and the turreted outline of Dudley Castle. T&S Element, formerly a well known BCN boat company, have premises overlooking Whimsey Bridge, but it is lorries they run these days, not narrowboats.

OLDBURY JUNCTION lies beneath the M5 motorway. This was the site of a boatyard belonging to another carrying company inseparable from the history of this area's canals. Thomas Clayton specialised in the transport of bulk liquids. Their boats had decked holes and were named after rivers. Numerous short haul traffics flourished on the BCN, primarily in the form of liquid wastes from gasworks, but Clayton's also carried as far afield as Ellesmere Port on the Shropshire Union Canal and Banbury on the Oxford Canal. The TITFORD CANAL, a real Black Country backwater full of unexpected charm and character, is described in our *Birmingham Canal Navigations* Canal Companion.

Playing hopscotch with the elevated sections of motorway, the old main line crosses Stewart Aqueduct, which offers a bird's eye view down on to the new main line, then reaches SPON LANE JUNCTION. In gloom cast by the concrete ceiling of the motorway, the canal twists between broad support columns reminiscent of a latter-day cathedral nave.

New Main Line

Whilst Brindley's canal winds about the foot of the Rowley Hills reciting poetry to itself, Telford's gets to grips with the business of reaching Birmingham in a no nonsense manner which your accountant would approve of. For almost three miles, the canal runs as true as a line on a balance sheet, crossing great open expanses of wasteland where large craters recall past quarrying and brickmaking. These areas have been designated for development as urban woodland; inexorably the *Black Country* is becoming *green* again, going full circle back to its pre-industrial origins. At DUDLEY PORT JUNCTION the Netherton Branch makes a bee-line for its famous tunnel. Opened in 1858 to relieve pressure on the parallel Dudley Tunnel, it was the last canal tunnel to be built in Britain, going into the record books, at 3027 yards, as the eighth longest.

Racing the trains – and not *always* losing, you come to ALBION JUNCTION and the Gower Branch link-up with the old main line and Wolverhampton Level. A former toll island all but fills the width of the new main line, an 'eye of the needle' job for nervous steerers. The big grey tanks of Bromford oil terminal border the cut, then it passes beneath the railway to reach PUDDING GREEN JUNCTION where Telford's improved route meets Brindley's original WEDNESBURY CANAL. Beneath the junction roving bridge the esoteric waters of the northern half of the BCN beckon. Venture down there and you may never be the same again. We did, and you can read how we lived to tell the tale in the *BCN Canal Companion*.

Steelworks overlook the canal as it reaches BROMFORD JUNCTION. Here it's decision time again; you can stay on Telford's route, or pass up the trio of locks in the Spon Lane flight to regain the old main line. The new main line keeps to the *Birmingham Level* and passes beneath the M5 and the Stewart Aqueduct, entering a vast cutting of blue-brick retaining walls between the railway on one side and Chance's glassworks on the other. Now all but defunct, the works produced over a million square feet of glazing for the Crystal Palace.

Oldbury

Redevelopment continues to alter the face of Oldbury, though here and there echoes of the old Worcestershire town bounce back at you. L.T.C. Rolt wrote: "Of Oldbury, with its mean, blackened streets, I can find no redeeming word to say," but then he had a horror of over industriali-sation, whereas a lot of us have an acute nostalgia for many aspects of it now. The vast conglomerate offices of Sandwell MBC's new civic headquarters now dominate the town, and the mind can only boggle at the army of bureaucrats employed in keeping tabs on the rest of us who actually have to make something useful in order to earn a living.

Eating & Drinking

WAGGON & HORSES – Church Street. Standing defiantly opposite the new civic offices, this CAMRA recom-mended pub has retained virtually all its Victorian charac-

Continued on page 24

Continued from page 23

ter. Dispenses many of the region's best local ales plus a cycle of other guest beers. Food usually available. 5 minutes walk from Whimsey Bridge on the old main line.
THE RAILWAY – adjacent Sandwell & Dudley railway station, near Bromford Lane Bridge on the new main line. Simple M&B local serving snacks.
McDONALDS – 'drive-in' outlet adjacent to Whimsey Bridge, no loop provided for the boat trade as yet.

Shopping

The best canalside choice in shops between Wolverhampton and Birmingham. The centre is most easily reached from the old main line, but little more than ½ mile from the new at Bromford. Branches of most banks, small market on Tue & Sat. Some nice Black Country butchers and bakers.

Public Transport

BUSES – bus station in the vicinity of Whimsey Bridge with information office and departures and arrivals from many parts of the Black Country. Tel: 021-200 2700.
TRAINS – Intercity and local services railhead, Sandwell & Dudley, is adjacent to Bromford Lane Bridge. Tel: 021-643 2711.

Continued from page 21

local hero; the VICTORIA CHIPPY stands opposite.

Shopping

A handy little shopping centre easily reached from either canal. There are Barclays, Lloyds and TSB banks and a fair range of shops including a Co-op and a branch of Firkins for those in dire need of a cream cake or two.

Places to Visit

BLACK COUNTRY MUSEUM – open daily Mar-Oct 10am-5pm (reduced hours and services during winter months). Admission charge. Tel: 021-557 9643. Open air museum of buildings and machinery. Tram rides to/from entrance to canalside 'town centre', restored boat dock and trips by electric boats into Dudley Tunnel and the 'Singing Cavern'. Secure overnight moorings for visiting boaters, access via Tipton Junction. Bus links with Tipton railway station; ask locally.

Galton Bridge, Smethwick

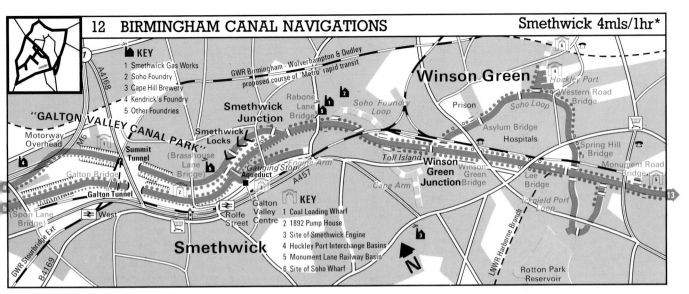

KEY
1 Smethwick Gas Works
2 Soho Foundry
3 Cape Hill Brewery
4 Kendrick's Foundry
5 Other Foundries

KEY
1 Coal Loading Wharf
2 1892 Pump House
3 Site of Smethwick Engine
4 Hockley Port Interchange Basins
5 Monument Lane Railway Basin
6 Site of Soho Wharf

REALISATION OF THE IMPACT made by Thomas Telford's new main line comes with exploration of the lengthy loops its superseded. By the end of the 18th century Brindley's canal had become a victim of its old success; water was short and traffic congested. Telford was called in to suggest improvements and discovered 'a canal little better than a crooked ditch'! The original towing path had deteriorated to the extent that horses frequently slid and staggered into the water, tow lines entangled when boats met, and boatmen quarrelled over precedence at the locks. Telford devised a bold improvement plan cutting through the Smethwick summit. The work took five years and was completed in 1829. It reduced the distance between Wolverhampton and Birmingham by a third. A local historian found the new route "unsurpassed in stupendous magnificence"!

It is difficult still not to be impressed by the puissance of Telford's engineering; though just as easy to be beguiled by Brindley's peregrinations. The old loops retained their local traffics, serving works firmly established along their banks. So the Oozells Street, Iknield Port and Soho (but not the Cape or Soho Foundry) loops remain navigable to this day,

functioning – as does a greater part of the BCN – as storm drainage channels and linear reservoirs for industry. Go on, try them!

Westwards from SMETHWICK JUNCTION the old and new main lines forge their separate routes to and from Tipton. The earlier canal ascends through three locks to reach its 473ft summit. Originally its course lay even higher (at 491ft) traces of which can be discerned along the embankment above the canal as its proceeds west of Brasshouse Lane Bridge. An even better viewpoint is the footbridge straddling the railway just west of Rolfe Street station. From here there's a grandstand view of the two main lines as they sweep past Smethwick, a scene without parallel anywhere else on the inland waterways system.

Access to the celebrated ENGINE ARM is through the tiny arch of a stone side bridge adjacent to Smethwick Top Lock. The arm spans the new main line by way of a wonderfully gothic iron bridge, a real treasure in the context of its industrial setting. On the far side of the aqueduct the arm turns a right angle past moorings for the Galton Valley Centre, a community project of restored warehouses often used as a meeting place by the

*Allow 2 hrs for Brindley's route with loops and locks.

Birmingham Canal Navigations Society. The navigable end of the arm is soon reached and there is no winding hole at the far end. It was built to serve as a feeder from Rotton Park Reservoir. If you scale the bank opposite the junction with the Soho Loop at Winson Green you can see the feeder running through a brick channel. The Engine Arm derives its name from James Watt's 'Smethwick Engine' of 1779 which was introduced to pump water up the original flight of six locks. Even when three of these were by-passed in 1790 the engine continued its work for another century until the pumping engine at Brasshouse Lane was commissioned. Watt's engine is now housed in the Museum of Science & Industry in Birmingham and is still occasionally steamed.

The 1892 Pump House has been refurbished by the local authority. West of here the old main line, running along the course engineered by Smeaton in 1790, penetrates an unexpected oasis of water plantin and rosebay willow herb. For a moment it is possible to make believe you are deep in the countryside, but any rural illusion is shattered by the affrontery of the so-called SUMMIT TUNNEL, an ugly concrete tube covered by the high embankment of a dual carriageway which mockingly bears Telford's name.

Beyond the tunnel the canal is embraced by a deep and swarthy cutting and overlooked by the high rises of West Bromwich. A derelict concrete structure was once used to load boats with coal brought by cable tramway from the Jubilee Colliery in Sandwell. The cutting, and any lingering buccolic fancies, come to an abrupt end as the canal is swallowed up beneath the elevated section of the M5.

Winson Green

Winson Green was one of the last areas of Birmingham to be urbanised at the end of the 18th century, but the pleasant sounding name struck dread into Brummagem folks' hearts, for here was the workhouse, the lunatic asylum and the gaol. The Great Western Railway built a vast goods yard and interchange basin at nearby Hockley Port, but now the tracks are gone and the basins have found new use as a youth centre for water-based activities and as an urban farm.

S O THIS IS BIRMINGHAM, centre, to all intents and purposes, of the inland waterways of England, and FARMER'S BRIDGE JUNCTION is the fulcrum of the Birmingham Canal Navigations. Overlooked by the International Convention Centre and the National Sports Arena, it reflects Birmingham's confidence in the future. All a far cry from the day, over two centuries ago, when, a certain Mr Farmer's land was bisected by the new inland waterway, and an accommodation bridge (long since demolished) erected to preserve his right of way.

In contrast to the old line's excursions over the summit, Telford's route lies in the shadows cast by extensive earthworks; dank corridors of blue engineering brick retaining walls and precipitous banks of bracken and bramble. The scale of these 19th century works, accomplished by navvies totally without sophisticated machinery, tends to be overwhelming. But the climax is Telford's majestic GALTON BRIDGE, hovering for all it's worth like a metallic falcon, seventy feet above the canal. Without recourse to hyperbole, it is simply one of the great bridges of Britain, and were it located anywhere else but Smethwick, would undoubtedly be recognised as such.

Between Smethwick and Winson Green the old and new main lines are one, sharing the same route through an industrial heartland of foundries and railway sidings. Much of the fun to be had from exploring the BCN derives from piecing together clues to its past. Near Rabone Lane Bridge Matthews Boulton and James Watt opened their Soho Foundry, the first factory in the world to be lit by gas so that work could continue after darkness had fallen. Visited by Boswell in 1776, Boulton boasted: 'I sell here, sir, what all the world desires to have – power!' Adjacent to the western junction of the SOHO LOOP (and again beneath the Engine Arm aqueduct) stand the bases of former island toll houses. These octagonally shaped offices were strategically sited to keep account of the numerous short-haul traffics which operated throughout the BCN. Now only the bases remain, which is a pity because old photographs show them to have been pretty little buildings – had one survived it would have made an ideal home for a canal based craft shop.

Smethwick

One side of the High Street was demolished to make way for a dual-carriageway and Smethwick has never really recovered from such a severe amputation. Shops are within easy reach of Brasshouse Lane Bridge via the railway footbridge, but quite honestly you would be better off pressing on to Birmingham or Oldbury.

They rang the church bells all day when the canal reached Birmingham and celebrations followed into the night. The first section, opened in 1769, linked Birmingham with the mines in Wednesbury, and it is said that the price of coal was halved. Interesting to reflect, then, that when the M40 motorway was extended from Oxford to the outskirts of Birmingham in 1990, no church bells were rung in such glee and no prices fell in the department stores of Corporation Street. Anyway, during the rest of the 18th century Birmingham became a magnet for canal promoters and, in 1794, the

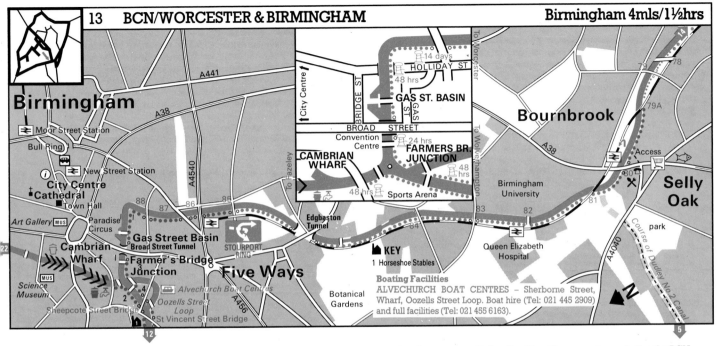

Birmingham Canal Navigations were formed, amounting to some 160 miles of waterway, of which 100 miles remain navigable in an area bounded by Wolverhampton, Walsall, Tamworth and Dudley.

There *were* celebrations, however, in 1991 when the International Convention Centre opened alongside the canal, and Birmingham here has something to be proud of. Delegates from all over the world are being wooed to convene in Birmingham instead of Brussels or Baltimore, and who knows what magic of the BCN may rub off on them. Passenger boats ply from the Convention Centre's doorstep offering a taster of the local canals, and for once the hackneyed analogy with Venice seems almost apt.

From the piazzas of the Convention Centre the canal leads through Broad Street Tunnel to GAS STREET BASIN, the epitome, and for many the soul, of Birmingham's waterways. In fact Gas Street has come to symbolise the BCN to such an extent that it is often forgotten that the actual terminal wharf and offices of the Birmingham Canal lay to the east of here, on a site now occupied by the skyscraper premises of Central Television. Two arms terminated at the rear of the BCN company's handsomely symmetrical offices on Suffolk Street which were sadly demolished in 1928. Demolition controversially took its toll of the Gas Street canalscape in 1975 as well, by which time the planners should have known better, and British Waterways have never really been forgiven for razing their rich heritage of 18th century waterside warehouses to the ground in a calculated move to sidestep a preservation order. And for a time nothing was done to fill the void. Gas Street might have ceased to exist but for a community of →

residential boats which lent a splash of colour and humanity to a decaying canalscape. A decade passed before the developer's proposals were realised in bricks and mortar, and the biggest irony of all is that the new pubs and offices were built in a warehouse vernacular style of remarkable likeness to the bulldozed originals. The only post Seventies interloper unsympathetic to the scale of the original Gas Street is the towering, shimmering, slippery, silvered edifice of the Hyatt Hotel. What do its sybaritic guests make of the little boats miles below their air-conditioned eyries; do they see them as 'local colour', as archaic as the sampans of Hong Kong harbour?

Work began on the WORCESTER & BIRMINGHAM CANAL from the Birmingham end in 1794, but it was not until 1815 that the route was completed throughout. Fearful of its water supply disappearing down into the Severn, the Birmingham Canal Company at first refused to be directly linked with the newcomer, and so laborious transhipment of through traffic took place across an infamous divide known as the 'Worcester Bar'. Eventually, however a stop lock was provided between the two waterways, to give the BCN some measure of protection, yet enabling through passage of boats.

South-westwards from GAS STREET the Worcester & Birmingham delves into the sylvan suburbs of Edgbaston. It was this cloistered, arboreous approach of the W&B into the city that prompted Robert Aickman to express the aphorism: 'Canals stretch green fingers into towns.' He might have added yellow and purple, for by late summer, the borders of the canal and the adjoining railway are a riot of rosebay willowherb and golden rod. This approach to, or exit from the second city always comes as a surprise to those making its acquaintance for the first time, and it is a route used more and more by pedestrians and cyclists in preference to the choked carriageways of the A38. A regular waterbus service between the Convention Centre, Birmingham University and Cadbury World at Bournville ought to be a viable proposition. Between bridges 81 and 82 the canal offers a panoramic view across the university campus with its startling Italianate tower. At SELLY OAK the Dudley No.2 Canal once joined up with the Worcester & Birmingham. Little trace of the junction can be discerned now, but west of the A4040 the course of the canal has been turned into a public footpath for a couple of miles, finishing just short of the famous tunnel at Lapal (see Map 5).

Birmingham

Canal boating holidays come low enough in the kudos stakes, and Birmingham as a destination lower still. But any sympathy that your friends can muster will be wasted. Let them bake on some beach. There is more character in Birmingham's big toe than the whole of 'The Med' put together. Since the opening of the International Convention Centre, moorings in the city centre have been formalised and put under the control of a Harbour Master based in the old toll office at Cambrian Wharf. The enlargement on Map 13 shows where you can moor and for how long. Prime site (24 hour maximum stay) is alongside the ICC itself, but space is limited and there are 48 hour alternatives alongside the National Sports Arena and by Holliday Street aqueduct.

From whichever mooring you choose, the city centre is only a few minutes walk away, and the metropolitan – not to say cosmopolitan character of the place may come as a surprise to those with preconceived notions of an ungainly, uncouth city where everyone speaks through their nose and has something to do with the making of motor cars. Cars, though, have lost their pole

position in the 'Brummagem' scheme of things, and as the years pass the city continues to recover from its crass submission to the needs of motor traffic which ruined it in the Sixties and Seventies. At the end of 1991 the city centre was given back to pedestrians, and for the first time in decades you can walk along New Street and Corporation Street without the accompaniment of the roar of traffic.

There are deeper oases of calm and character to be discovered too. Churches like St Philip's Cathedral and St Paul's, the 'Jeweller's Church'; museums like the Art Gallery and the Science Museum; proud civic buildings like the Town Hall and the Council House; the bustling markets of the Bull Ring; and quiet backwaters of the Jewellery Quarter. These are the bits of Birmingham you should make it your business to see.

Eating & Drinking

Pubs, restaurants and wine bars gather around Gas Street Basin like wasps on a cream bun, drawing inspiration from the verisimilitude of the setting, and bearing suitably utilitarian names like THE WHARF, THE BRASSHOUSE,

and THE GLASS WORKS, but not – in our opinion – providing the kind of ambience most canallers are likely to warm to after a hard day's boating. Similarly, the JAMES BRINDLEY apes the architecture of the past, pays homage to the canal in its decor, and can be a haven of quiet on a slow lunchtime, but tends towards noise at night. In contrast, the PRINCES OF WALES on Cambridge Street (rear of Repertory Theatre and ICC), provides the authenticity of a tradtional city centre pub.

All the establishments overlooking Gas Street provide food of one sort or another, but for a quieter setting, try the ethnic restaurants of Fletcher Walk (reached by walking along Broad Street towards the city centre) through the underpass by the TSB bank) like the Spanish CASA PACO and Italian LATINO, where you can consol yourselves with a taste of the Mediterranean if you have had a wet week in the Black Country instead. In the nearby Paradise Forum ROSSINIS also provide Italian fare, whilst across Chamberlain Square, the EDWARDIAN TEA ROOMS in the Art Gallery serve coffees, light lunches and teas in splendid gothic surroundings at modest prices and, if you've timed it right, the resident pianist

Continued on page 48

River Severn at Worcester

Town & Country
Top left: BCN Main Line between Coseley and Tipton
Lower left: Barker Bridge on the Birmingham & Fazeley Canal
Above: The Stourbridge Canal from Primrose Hill
Right: The Trent Valley at Colwich

Main picture: Shortwood Tunnel, Worcester & Birmingham Canal
Opposite left: Gas Street Basin, Birmingham
Top left: ICC, Birmingham
Top right: Top Lock, Wolverhampton
Right: Kidderminster Lock

Sunbathing in the Black Country

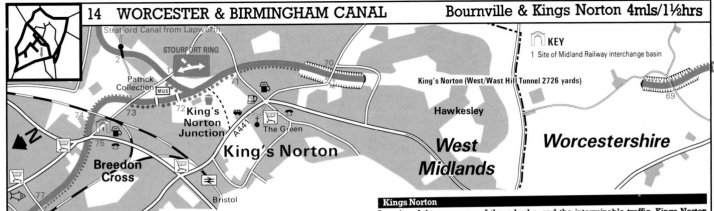

THE RICH AROMA of chocolate heralds Bournville and Cadbury's famous factory. This is your chance to visit CADBURY WORLD and unwrap the secrets of chocolate making down the centuries. Cadburys had close connections with the canals. They operated their own fleet of narrowboats, and where modern housing now lines the canal north of bridge 77, there once stood extensive wharves connected to the main works on the opposite bank of the canal by a private railway system.

Another tourist attraction lies beside Kings Norton Junction where a former paper mill has been converted to house THE PATRICK COLLECTION of classic motor cars. The Stratford Canal joins the Worcester & Birmingham at Kings Norton and, if you haven't ever explored this particular canal, it's worth a short detour along the towpath to see the curious former guillotine stop lock which once separated the water supplies of the two companies.

Kings Norton Tunnel (sometimes known as Wast or even West Hill) takes about half an hour to pass through and, although clearances can be deceptive, it is possible to pass oncoming craft inside its gloomy depths. As your eyes become accustomed to daylight again you'll notice the scene shifters have been at work: southbound the rural delights of Worcestershire await your appreciation; northbound you find yourself being sucked into the suburbs of the 'Second City'.

Kings Norton

In spite of the pressures of the suburbs, and the interminable traffic, Kings Norton retains a fragile village feel, enhanced by the survival of the (possibly pre-Norman) green. 'The Mop', a former hiring fair with its origins steeped in the Middle Ages, is still held on the first Monday in October. Enthusiasts of church architecture will want to visit the impressive 14th century church. Tucked away in a shadowy corner of the graveyard lurks the half-timbered old Grammar School. Grouped about the village green are numerous useful shops (including chemist, launderette, delicatessen, off licence and Lloyd's Bank) a Chinese take away and an Indian restaurant. Frequent buses head for Birmingham, as do trains from the station ½ mile north along the A441.

Things to Do

CADBURY WORLD – Linden Road, Bournville, Birmingham B30 2LU. Tel: 021-433 4334. Access from moorings alongside Bournville railway station. Go through the gate on to the platform and follow the way out sign through the subway. The entrance to the visitor centre is just a few yards from the station. Cadbury World is open daily and there is an admission charge. Inside the origins of chocolate are traced, the development of Cadbury's family business, the company's long success with advertising & publicity and – of special interest to canal fans – the transport of raw materials and finished products. Modern day production techniques are highlighted as well and, naturally, there is a gift shop dispensing edible souvenirs of your visit. THE PATRICK COLLECTION – 180 Lifford Lane, Kings Norton. Tel: 021-459 9111. Visitor moorings north of bridge 72. Open daily during school and bank holidays, plus Wed, Sat & Sun end March to end October. Admission charge. Exciting 'museum' of motor and racing cars imaginatively displayed int two exhibition halls along with authentic period settings. Restaurant, cafeteria, landscaped grounds, souvenir shop and children's play area.

THE CANAL WORMS its secluded way around the hillside above Alvechurch. There are panoramic views eastwards over windmill-topped Weatheroak Hill, crossed by the Roman's Ryknild Street. A feeder comes in from Upper Bittell reservoir beside an isolated canal employee's cottage near bridge 66. The Lower reservoir, rich in wildfowl, lies alongside the canal and has a gorgeous wooded backdrop crowned by the Lickey Hills. Only the Upper reservoir feeds the canal. The Lower was provided by the canal company to compensate millers in the vicinity whose water supplies from the River Arrow had been affected by construction of the canal. In 1985 a short section of the canal was re-routed to accommodate construction of the M42 motorway. The old course of the canal disappears beneath bridge 64A. Bridge 62 carries the electrified, 'Cross-City' commuter line which links Redditch with Lichfield. The trip down to Redditch through the countryside of the Arrow Valley from Alvechurch's tiny station makes for an enjoyable excursion 'ashore'.

The odour of wild garlic is so pronounced, and the oak and alder so enveloping, that passing through the approach cuttings to Shortwood Tunnel is like being embraced by an over enthusiastic Frenchman; all that's missing is the tang of Galouise. As with all other Worcester & Birmingham tunnels (except for Edgbaston) the towpath doesn't go through the tunnel. In working boat days the horses were led over the top and here the path remains well defined. Not so, however, the towpath between the southern portal of Shortwood and the northern of Tardebigge, which is so overgrown and eroded for much of this length as to be unwalkable. Nevertheless it is pleasant to wander across the tunnel tops, daydreaming perhaps that you are leading a boat horse whilst your cargo makes its subterranean way through the earth beneath your feet, hauled by one of the erstwhile tunnel tugs which were such a feature of this section of canal.

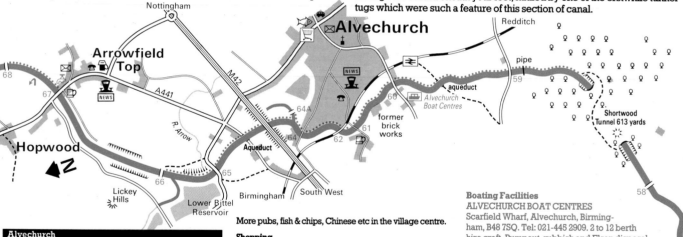

Alvechurch

Eating & Drinking

THE CROWN – canalside bridge 61. Hospitable M&B pub offering excellent and inexpensive bar meals. Boaters club open at rear during cruising season.

More pubs, fish & chips, Chinese etc in the village centre.

Shopping

There is a good range of shops in the village centre (inc: Midland & Lloyds banks, chemist, butcher, off licence, food stores etc) but it is a long climb back to the canal. Provisions are much more handily obtained at the Boat Centre's shop.

Boating Facilities

ALVECHURCH BOAT CENTRES
Scarfield Wharf, Alvechurch, Birmingham, B48 7SQ. Tel: 021-445 2909. 2 to 12 berth hire craft. Pumpout, rubbish and Elsan disposal, water, diesel, repairs & servicing, slipway Calor gas, sales & brokerage, moorings, white storage, payphones and excellent shop with gifts, books and provisions. Members of the Blue Riband Club.

TARDEBIGGE LOCKS represents a boater's Rite of Passage. Once you have tackled this flight which, taken with the neighbouring six at Stoke, amount to thirty-six locks in four miles, other groups of locks seem small beer. The Thirty chambers of the Tardebigge flight raise the canal 217 feet; the top lock being, at 14 feet, one of the deepest narrowbeam locks on the system. Happily the flight is in good condition, and the lock-wheeler has time to appreciate the stunning views offered towards the Malvern Hills.

Tardebigge itself holds a special place in the story of the inland waterways movement. It was here that Robert Aickman made his way from Bromsgrove station to meet Tom and Angela Rolt aboard their narrowboat home, *Cressy*, which had been moored above the top lock throughout the war. As a direct result of their meeting the Inland Waterways Association was formed. A plinth adjacent to the lock tells the story, though there is some debate as to whether their first meeting took place in 1946, as stated, or in the previous year.

Tom Rolt painted vivid pictures of the canal at Tardebigge in two of his books: "Worcestershire", published by Robert Hale in 1949, and "Landscape with Canals", by Allen Lane in 1977. Another portrait of the canalside community appeared in "Lock Keeper's Daughter" by Pat Warner (Shepperton Swan 1986). All three books give the impression of an unchanging pattern of life centred on the canal and its trade, peopled by a cast of tug captains, reservoir keepers and lockgate makers. From the vantage point of the Nineties it seems an idyllic way of life, but there is still a welcome timelessness about Tardebigge which makes visiting here a rewarding experience.

Tardebigge

There are no shops or pubs within easy walking reach of the canal. The old Engine House by bridge 55 – once employed in back-pumping water from the reservoir to the summit – is now a restaurant and night-club; telephone Bromsgrove 35238 for reservations. Midland Red West buses operate hourly Mon-Sat from stops adjacent to the southern portal of the tunnel to Bromsgrove and Redditch.

Stoke Prior

Canalside pubs at bridges 44 and 48; THE NAVIGATION and QUEEN'S HEAD respectively. The latter is a particularly popular port of call for boaters, being highly regarded for its bar and restaurant meals. JAN'S KITCHEN (bridge 44) is open daily throughout the summer months for breakfasts and lunches. Evening meals can be arranged by appointment on Bromsgrove 79726. Less than a mile west of bridge 48 lies AVONCROFT, an outdoor museum of buildings – one of its exhibits, a weatherboarded windmill, can be glimpsed from the canal. Its open daily throughout the summer and on selected days during the winter. Tel: Bromsgrove (0527) 31886 for further details.

Boating Facilities

DARTLINE – Old Wharf, Tardebigge, Bromsgrove, Worcs. Tel: Bromsgrove (0527) 73898. 2 to 12 berth hire craft. Pumpout, diesel, Elsan & rubbish disposal, water, moorings, gift shop and payphone.

BLACK PRINCE HOLIDAYS – Stoke Prior, Bromsgrove, Worcs B60 4LA. Tel: Bromsgrove (0527) 575115. 2 to 10 berth hire craft. Pumpout, Elsan & rubbih disposal, water, diesel, gas, moorings.

NOWADAYS, BRITAIN'S SALT industry is largely confined to Cheshire but, as the name Droitwich suggests, this part of Worcestershire was once a centre of salt making too. The salt obsessed Romans built a special road between Droitwich and Alcester to carry this valuable commodity. Its course crosses the canal at Hanbury Wharf. Several thousand years later the Worcester & Birmingham built the short Droitwich Junction Canal from here down into the town to carry the same cargo. Barely two miles long, it included seven locks and passed briefly into the River Salwarpe before meeting the previously established Droitwich Canal at Vines Park near the centre of the town. Both of the Droitwich canals were derelict before the Second World War, but in recent years they have undergone varying degrees of restoration. At Hanbury Wharf the top pound of the Junction Canal has been re-watered and is in use as private moorings. A trip boat operates out of Droitwich along the summit of the wide beam Droitwich Canal

At the end of the 18th century, John Corbett, the son of a local boatman, discovered large deposits of brine beneath the surface at Stoke Prior and subsequently built a salt works on the site. It made his fortune. He married a French woman and built her a replica chateau in the nearby Worcestershire countryside, and he was in the forefront of the development of Droitwich as a spa town. Unfortunately, Droitwich's salt trade was killed off by the machinations of 'The Salt Union', a trade cartel which backfired on many of its members. The salt works at Stoke has long been closed.

Railway and canal join forces again beside the Astwood flight, and drift lazily through pleasant farmland. From the Bottom Lock (No.17) a footpath leads across the fields to Hanbury Hall, a National Trust property open to the public. Westwards there are views towards the Abberley Hills and, nearer by, the tall radio masts at Wychbold, a transmitting station dating from the early Thirties whose call sign was 'Droitwich Calling'. The masts may be demolished in the near future.

Stoke Works

Prosaically named after the enormous salt works now largely demolished and replaced by a high-tech pharmaceutical factory.

Eating & Drinking

THE BOWLING GREEN – ¼ mile west of bridge 41. Banks's, food, garden & bowls.
BOAT & RAILWAY – canalside bridge 42. Hanson's, snacks, skittle alley, customer moorings.

Shopping

Small food shop, open Thur-Sat & Sun am.

Public Transport

BUSES – Midland Red West to/from Droitwich & Bromsgrove Mon – Sat. Tel: Bromsgrove (0527) 72265. This approximately bi-hourly service passes close to Avoncroft Museum on its way to Bromsgrove.

Hanbury Wharf

Eating and Drinking

EAGLE & SUN – adjacent bridge 35. M&B beers and bar meals.

Boating Facilities

SARABAND – Hanbury Wharf, Droitwich, Worcs WR9 7DU. Tel: Droitwich (0905) 771018. Diesel, water, Calor gas, repairs & servicing, boatbuilding, sales & brokerage, slipway, payphone, chandlery and groceries.

THE CANAL SKIRTS the mellow settlements of Shernal Green, Dunhampstead, Oddingley and Tibberton. In spite of being sandwiched by the motorway and the railway, the waterway seems remote. High clumps of sedge border the canal, swaying with the passage of each boat and somehow emphasising the loneliness of the landscape. Occasionally a by-road crosses the canal, wandering eastwards into an empty tract of countryside which was once part of the Royal Forest of Feckenham. Incidentally, the River Avon is only a dozen miles away from here as the crow flies.

At 236 yards, Dunhampstead tunnel is the shortest of the five on this canal. Towpath walkers must leave or rejoin the canal at bridge 30 and use the adjacent country road, because the towpath no longer extends to the southern portal of the tunnel. Oddingley consists of little more than an ancient half-timbered house, a tiny church and a level-crossing keeper's house and

cabin. Tibberton, on the other hand, is a long straggling village of mostly modern housing. Offerton Locks lie in a pretty setting, if you can mentally ignore the electricity pylons and the motorway. The big farm by bridge 24 has some gorgeous weather-boarded barns.

Two aspects of the Worcester & Birmingham Canal's working practice were remarkable. Boats kept left when passing each other and pairs of donkeys were widely used in place of horses to haul the boats. Apparently the animals worked well together as long as they 'knew' each other, but the introduction of a new donkey could cause considerable ructions. One of the last traders on the canal was Charles Ballinger of Gloucester. He was still using horse-drawn boats as late as 1954, carrying coal from the Cannock area to Townsend's mill at Diglis. Occasionally he would have an 'uphill' cargo too: matches from Gloucester to Birmingham, or flour from Worcester to Tipton; but by the beginning of the Sixties trade had deserted the canal.

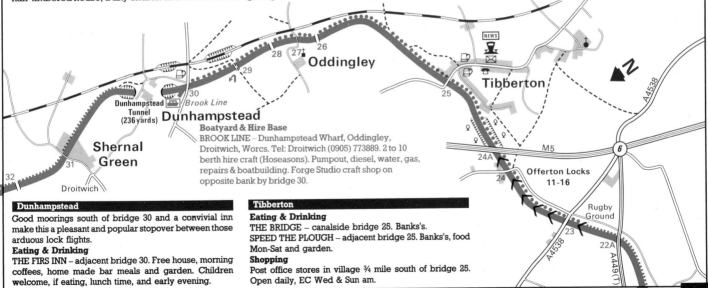

Dunhampstead

Good moorings south of bridge 30 and a convivial inn make this a pleasant and popular stopover between those arduous lock flights.

Eating & Drinking

THE FIRS INN – adjacent bridge 30. Free house, morning coffees, home made bar meals and garden. Children welcome, if eating, lunch time, and early evening.

Tibberton

Eating & Drinking

THE BRIDGE – canalside bridge 25. Banks's.

SPEED THE PLOUGH – adjacent bridge 25. Banks's, food Mon-Sat and garden.

Shopping

Post office stores in village ¾ mile south of bridge 25. Open daily, EC Wed & Sun am.

Boatyard & Hire Base

BROOK LINE – Dunhampstead Wharf, Oddingley, Droitwich, Worcs. Tel: Droitwich (0905) 773889. 2 to 10 berth hire craft (Hoseasons). Pumpout, diesel, water, gas, repairs & boatbuilding. Forge Studio craft shop on opposite bank by bridge 30.

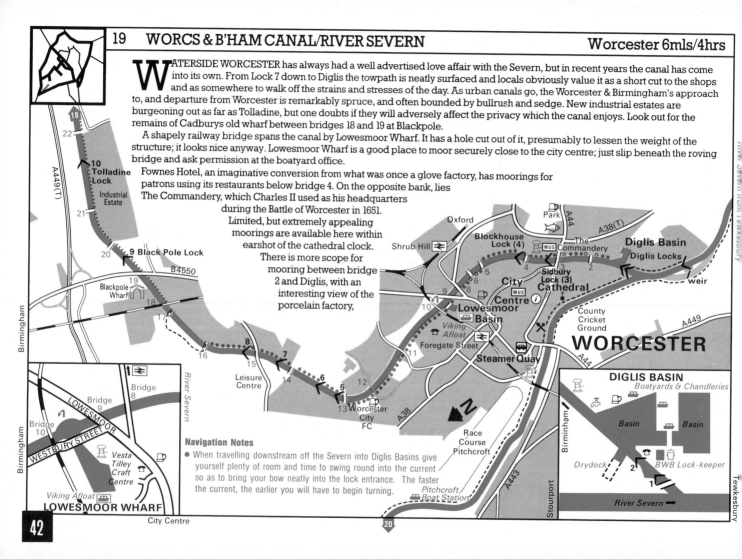

WATERSIDE WORCESTER has always had a well advertised love affair with the Severn, but in recent years the canal has come into its own. From Lock 7 down to Diglis the towpath is neatly surfaced and locals obviously value it as a short cut to the shops and as somewhere to walk off the strains and stresses of the day. As urban canals go, the Worcester & Birmingham's approach to, and departure from Worcester is remarkably spruce, and often bounded by bullrush and sedge. New industrial estates are burgeoning out as far as Tolladine, but one doubts if they will adversely affect the privacy which the canal enjoys. Look out for the remains of Cadburys old wharf between bridges 18 and 19 at Blackpole.

A shapely railway bridge spans the canal by Lowesmoor Wharf. It has a hole cut out of it, presumably to lessen the weight of the structure; it looks nice anyway. Lowesmoor Wharf is a good place to moor securely close to the city centre; just slip beneath the roving bridge and ask permission at the boatyard office.

Fownes Hotel, an imaginative conversion from what was once a glove factory, has moorings for patrons using its restaurants below bridge 4. On the opposite bank, lies The Commandery, which Charles II used as his headquarters during the Battle of Worcester in 1651. Limited, but extremely appealing moorings are available here within earshot of the cathedral clock. There is more scope for mooring between bridge 2 and Diglis, with an interesting view of the porcelain factory,

Navigation Notes

● When travelling downstream off the Severn into Diglis Basins give yourself plenty of room and time to swing round into the current so as to bring your bow neatly into the lock entrance. The faster the current, the earlier you will have to begin turning.

DIGLIS BASIN
Boatyards & Chandlers
Basin | Basin
Drydock
BWB Lock-keeper
River Severn →

LOWESMOOR WHARF

whose workforce have a distinctly earthy sense of humour. DIGLIS BASINS were opened in the 19th century to facilitate transhipment of cargoes between river and canal. These days they are full of boats familiar with the slap of saltwater on their bottoms. The basins are a great place for wandering inquisitively amidst the smell of paint and tar, and the noise of wood being sawn and metal being bent into shape.

Two broad locks separate the basins from the river. They are closed at night and don't open again until about eight in the morning, when the lock-keeper comes on duty. In most cases he doesn't get involved in operating the locks, but it's good to know he's around if you need his help or advice. Entering or leaving the river can pose problems, especially when the current is fast, and getting your crew on or off for the locks needs careful consideration. Downstream there is a *third* Diglis Lock, in fact an automated pair, as the Severn heads for Gloucester, a route covered by our "Severn & Avon Companion". Upstream, Sabrina flows beneath the great west window of the Cathedral and past antiquated wharves and warehouses beneath Worcester Bridge. On summer weekends a ferry operates in the vicinity of the Cathedral, and trip boats ply this reach as well, so keep a weather eye open for sudden manoeuvres. Limited official moorings are available on the city side between the road and rail bridges. Some boaters, though, are brazen enough to tie up to tree boles in front of the Cathedral itself.

Worcester

Descending from Birmingham to Worcester, the West Midlands are intuitively left behind, and you find yourself in streets were the *patois* has a distinctly West Country burr. Royal Worcester suffered more than most at the hands of the developers during the Sixties (Ian Nairn, the late architectural writer and broadcaster, was incensed) but much making of amends has been done in recent years to enhance the city's fabric. The Cathedral, gazing devoutly out over the Severn, belongs – along with Gloucester and Hereford – to a golden triangle of ecclesiastical paragons which share, each in turn over three years, Europe's oldest music festival, 'The Three Choirs'. From the deep well of Worcester's history you can draw inspiration from almost any era that catches your imagination. This was the 'faithful city' of the Civil War from which Charles II escaped following the final defeat of the Cavaliers. It was the home, for much of his life, of Sir Edward Elgar. Home too of the manufacturers of Royal Worcester porcelain and that ensign of the empire, Lea & Perrins sauce. And here you'll find one of the country's loveliest cricketing venues, Worcestershire's New Road ground.

Eating & Drinking

LITTLE SAUCE FACTORY – London Road. Little Pub Co establishment celebrating Worcester's saucy past. Excellent food and the usual eccentric atmosphere. Located just uphill from McTaffish by Sidbury Lock.
CADENCE CAFE – Foregate Street Station. A station buffet with a difference. Sandwiches cut freshly while you watch. Delicious cakes which they're not averse to serving with a dollop of ice cream. You can 'eat in', or

'take-away'. It may have to be the latter, for there is barely room to brandish a Bradshaw amidst the half dozen or so prettily laid tables. Open from 8 in the morning until the teatime train to Hereford. Cadence also hire out a range of bicycles and provide packed lunches and itineraries for exploration of the local countryside. Tel: Worcester (0905) 613501.
TILLEY'S BRASSERIE – City Walls Road. Part of Fownes Hotel. Limited customer moorings between bridges 3 and 4. All-day eatery named after locally born music hall star Vesta Tilley.
McTAFFISH – London Road. Spick & span, fish & chip parlour easily reached from bridge 3.

Shopping

Worcester is an excellent city in which to shop. Two refurbished shopping areas are The Hopmarket and

LOCK-KEEPERS HOUSE, DIGLIS.

Crown Passage. The Shambles, Friar Street and New Street feature numerous fascinating little shops and small businesses. If you are making the mistake of passing through non-stop by boat, then a number of useful provisions shops can be reached from bridge 3, by the Commandery.

Places to Visit

TOURIST INFORMATION CENTRE – The Guildhall, High Street. Tel: Worcester (0902) 726311. Worcester seems to have more visitor centres than any other provincial city of its size. A thorough list defeats us, but obvious highlights are THE COMMANDERY (canalside by Sidbury Lock) which was Charles II's headquarters during the Civil War; ROYAL WORCESTER (Severn Street, near Sidbury Lock again) the porcelain and bone china makers; and THE CATHEDRAL, dating from the 11th century and the burial place of King John.

Public Transport

BUSES – Midland Red West services throughout the area and local Citibus services. Tel: Worcester (0905) 23296 & 24898.
TRAINS – stations at Foregate Street and Shrub Hill. Services to/from The Malverns (nice idea for an excursion!) Birmingham, Kidderminster and London. Tel: (0452) 529501.

Boating Facilties

VIKING AFLOAT – Lowesmoor Wharf, Worcester WR1 2RX. Tel: Worcester (0905) 28667. 2 to 10 berth hire craft. Pumpout, rubbish & Elsan disposal, water, diesel, gas, payphone and souvenir shop. Secure casual moorings.

MAKE THE MOST of your brief encounter with the Severn, for unless you choose to tie up, perhaps – if there is room – at Bevere or Holt locks, or at one of the riparian hostelries – like the "Camp House" or "The Hampstall" – the three or four hours spent on the river between Worcester and Stourport are apt to flash swiftly by, leaving you with just a treasured blur of alder and willow fringed banks broken by occasional outcrops of sandstone; caravan parks and static homes; cattle or anglers flank or thigh high in the river margin; and the unruffled routine of the automated locks.

At Bevere Lock the keeper is so in love with his job that he spends a good proportion of his wages on the upkeep of the gorgeous lock-side gardens; a profusion of hanging baskets, flower tubs, conifers and cacti. The effect is so delightful that Bevere has become the Liverpool of lock-keeping, and the incumbent, Donald Smith, who first took up residence at Bevere in 1964, has won the coveted National best kept lock competition with a regularity that must be the despair of would be rivals.

A loop in the river forms the three acre island of Bevere, a place of refuge for the good burghers of Worcester in medieval times when war or plague threatened. Just upstream, the little River Salwarpe makes a mouse like entrance from the east, having risen on the slopes of the Lickey Hills and wound down through Bromsgrove and Droitwich to meet the Severn. Alongside, between two houses mostly hidden by foliage, lie the remains of the bottom lock of the Droitwich Canal opened in 1771. Surveyed by **Brindley**, though actually engineered by John Priddey, the canal flourished during the 19th century as an export route for the salt industry, an activity carried out in the vicinity of Droitwich since Roman times. When salt making declined this 'barge' canal fell into decay and was disused by the time of the first world war. In 1973 a trust was formed to restore the canal and the summit pound and a sizeable basin in central Droitwich have been returned to water. Recent research trips, though, suggest that the scheme may be moribund; temporarily one hopes.

The village of Grimley sits well back from the river, though anglers make use of the bumpy lane down to the water's edge to reach their perches in amongst the musky clumps of balsam. Napoleon's brother, Lucien Bonaparte, lived nearby in exile for a period of time. The public footpath which has accompanied the west bank of the Severn up from Worcester ends abruptly opposite Hawford at the site of a long abandoned ferry.

Summary of Facilities

Only the CAMP HOUSE INN slakes the thirst of Severn boaters and anglers. There are moorings for patrons (albeit limited) below Bevere Lock. The beer is Flowers and they do bar meals at lunchtimes and early in the evening daily except for Sunday. Children are well catered for. Up at the lock, the keeper runs a small gift shop offering ice cream and pop as well.

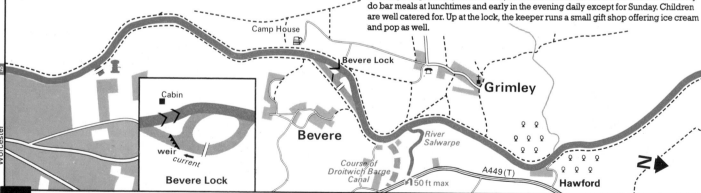

"**A**NYONE SO DISPOSED could forget the present in Shrawley Woods", wrote L.T.C. Rolt ("Worcestershire", Robert Hale, 1949), going on to evoke two halycon summer days moored on *Cressy* along this most beautiful of upper navigable Severn reaches between Holt and Lincomb locks. Disregard for the present presupposes a nostalgia for the past, and it is intriguing to discover that Dick Brook – emerging almost imperceptibly out of the shadowy trees on the western bank – was once made navigable in the 17th century to serve a forge located deep in the woods. Two or three lock chambers were cut out of the sandstone, and barges trading up from the Forest of Dean, conveyed cargoes of pig iron along the narrow stream to the doors of the forge.

The Severn acts like a magnet to West Midlanders seeking solace from their urban environment. A rash of caravan parks, and shanty-like chalets mar otherwise unspoilt riverside meadows for everyone but their proud owners. Luckily, this manifestation of mankind's capacity for destroying the very tranquility he desires is confined to those parts of the river nearest main roads. Holt Fleet is such a place, apt to bristle with 'Brummies' on sunny weekends, and yet Telford's dignified bridge of 1827, the resplendent lock, and the tumbling woods on the southern bank, do much to dissipate their intrusion. At least you, the boater can escape up or down stream to more secluded reaches. They, poor sods, have got to fight their way through the traffic all the way home.

Before Telford's bridge was built travellers crossed the river at Holt by ferry. Trace your finger down an old map of the Severn and you'll discover a sad litany of forgotten water crossings between Stourport and Worcester: Redstone, Cloth House, Hampstall, Lenchford, Hawford, Camp, Kepax and Pitchcroft. Alas the idyllic and (to anyone ever charmed by H.G. Wells' account of 'Mr Polly's' sojourn at the "Potwell Inn") enviable lifestyle of the ferrymen came to an end once people replaced Sunday afternoon rambles along the riverbank with a drive in a motor car. Not that there wasn't a darker side to ferrying. In 1919 the Hampstall ferry at The Burf was swamped by the waves of a passing steamer, and sunk drowning nine people.

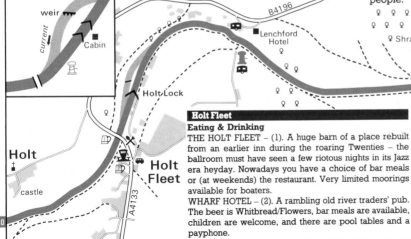

Holt Fleet

Eating & Drinking
THE HOLT FLEET – (1). A huge barn of a place rebuilt from an earlier inn during the roaring Twenties – the ballroom must have seen a few riotous nights in its Jazz era heyday. Nowadays you have a choice of bar meals or (at weekends) the restaurant. Very limited moorings available for boaters.

WHARF HOTEL – (2). A rambling old river traders' pub. The beer is Whitbread/Flowers, bar meals are available, children are welcome, and there are pool tables and a payphone.

Shopping
Two general stores open daily. The furthest from the river does Calor gas.

Public Transport
BUSES – Midland Red West services Mon-Sat to/from Worcester & Kidderminster. Tel: Worcester (0905) 23296.

The Burf

Eating & Drinking
THE HAMPSTALL INN – riverside, customer moorings. Bar meals; children welcome.

THE BLACK COUNTRY RING.

WITH 24 LOCKS in 2½ miles, the BIRMINGHAM & FAZELEY'S departure from (or approach to) Birmingham makes considerable demands on the boater's reservoir of energy: four or five hours hard graft amongst the design studios and tower blocks of the Farmer's Bridge flight and the remorseless redevelopments of the Aston 'Heartlands'. Furthermore the towpath of the 'Old Thirteen' is such a popular promenade nowadays, that any operation of the locks is likely to be a well-publicised affair, and you are apt to be accompanied, like a tournament golfer, by a crowd of onlookers from chamber to chamber. These FARMER'S BRIDGE LOCKS are an object lesson in urban regeneration. A decade ago they were a largely inaccessible, run-down eyesore, a boil on Birmingham's bottom, suffering from years of neglect following the demise of commercial carrying in the early Sixties. In 1984 a programme of renewal got under way sponsored by the Birmingham Inner City Partnership. Using Gas Street to Aston Junction as a prototype, BICP set about resurfacing the towpath, improving and increasing access, landscaping, lighting and general restoration at a cost of a cool million. The scheme's impact was considerable. It introduced Brummies to a well-kept secret aspect of their city, and they came to discover it in droves; so that now it hooches with shop and office staff on warm weekday lunchtimes and family groups on postprandial Sunday walks. The joggers relish it too, extending their limbs and expending their energy up and down the ribbed

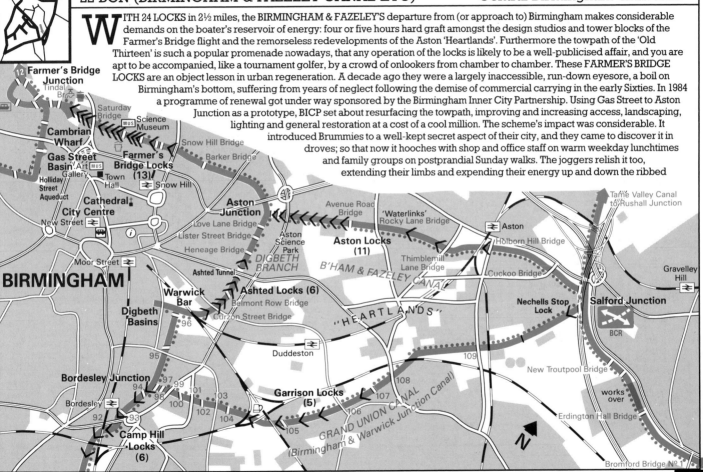

*Time & distance refer to Farmer's Bridge – Salford Junction section.

brick surfaces of the refurbished towpath in a distant echo of the hurrying boatmen of the past.

The canal environment at ASTON JUNCTION highlights the degree of change that the BCN canalscape has undergone in recent years. Contrast the concrete bulk of the Aston Expressway with the delicate ironwork of the Horseley roving bridge which spans the top lock. The DIGBETH BRANCH threads its way from here through the high-tech offices and laboratories of Aston Science Park on its way down the Ashted flight to WARWICK BAR and the Grand Union Canal.

ASTON LOCKS carrying the canal through a long established industrial area. Numerous side bridges indicate what an important part the waterway played in bringing raw materials into these factories and taking finished products and waste away. Nowadays the canal's role is more cosmetic, as evinced by the office development by Rocky Lane Bridge which is provided with its own little pastiche of a canal. For the time being, though, there is still enough canalside industrialisation in Aston and Nechells to remind us that the canal was dug to generate business, and if Farmer's Bridge locks are gregarious, Aston's still have more of an affinity with Greta Garbo. Even though the towpath has been resurfaced, pedestrians and joggers seem loath to venture this far from the city centre; the only sign of humanity – if that is the right category of species - being the graffiti scrawled on every available surface.

An aqueduct over the turgid River Tame carries the canal to SALFORD JUNCTION, a meeting place of three canals, which gather like a street gang striking poses beneath the concrete canopy of Spaghetti Junction. From here the Tame Valley section of the BCN heads off northwards in the general direction of Walsall, whilst the BIRMINGHAM & WARWICK JUNCTION branch of the Grand Union Canal provides a link with Bordesley and the main canal route to London. The ASTON - SALFORD section of the Birmingham & Fazeley Canal is the obvious, most expedient departure from, and approach to, Birmingham for travellers doing THE BLACK COUNTRY RING, but the detour via Bordesley and Warwick Bar is an entertaining alternative of likely appeal to diehard canal fans and students of industrial archaeology. Not that it is one which they could have cruised in recent years, for it has been closed to navigation since 1987, a victim of vandalism and, it has to be said, indifferent maintenance. As we went to press the opinion was that it would re-open in 1992. Fuller descriptions of its dubious charms appear in our BCN and SOUTH MIDLANDS Canal companions.

South-westwards from Salford Junction the Birmingham & Fazeley Canal is crypt engulfed by industry, at one point passing through a gloomy cavity caused by the extension of a works over the top of the canal. New Troutpool Bridge mocks at the 20th century environment we have created for ourselves. There are no trout in the highly polluted River Tame now, which churns turgidly through its man made channel beneath the elevated motorway.

Continued from page 28

or string trio will be on hand to aid the digestive juices. Towards the city centre the scope widens beyond the space available here to digest, but we would mention ATKINSON'S BAR (part of the Midland Hotel and approached from Stephenson Street opposite The Pallasades) which dispenses a decent pint of Holdens and other guest beers along with lunchtime snacks in a 'gentlemen's club' sort of atmosphere.

Shopping
The Bull Ring markets – indoor and out – are a famous focal point of Midland merchandising. In nearby Edgbaston Street, the 'Rag Market' (Tue, Fri & Sat) is the place for bargains. The Bull Ring shopping centre and the Pallasades above New Street station are predictable precincts, but the Pavilions development in High Street is imaginative and rewarding, even if you are only window shopping. New Street and Corporation Street burgeon with department stores and multiple chains. Canallers in a hurry – if that's not a contradiction in terms – will find a useful general store adjacent to Tindal Bridge by Cambrian Wharf. Across the canal from the ICC, Brindley Place was in the early throes of development as we went to press. The developers paid a cool £23 million for the site and will want their money's worth in the way of retail giants.

Places to Visit
INTERNATIONAL CONVENTION CENTRE – Broad Street. Tel: 021-200 2000. Even if you are not a delegate, worth a visit to take in its confident new architecture. Light meals and snacks available from the "Quayside Cafe" along with boat trips for those not already on the water. CBSO concerts, and other musical events in the Symphony Hall.
NATIONAL SPORTS ARENA – King Edward's Road. Tel: 021-200 2202. New "world class" indoor venue for sport overlooking Farmer's Bridge Junction.
MUSEUM & ART GALLERY – Chamberlain Square. Open daily, admission free. Tel: 021-235 2834.
MUSEUM OF SCIENCE & INDUSTRY – Newhall Street. Open daily, admission free. Tel: 021-236 1022. Convenient access by lock 9 on Farmer's Bridge flight.
CENTRAL LIBRARY – Chamberlain Square. Tel: 021-235 4511. The well stocked Library Shop is of particular interest to visitors with its wide range of local publications and souvenirs.
TOURIST INFORMATION – City Arcade (off Corporation Street). Tel: 021-643 2514. Branch desk at ICC.

Public Transport
Local bus & train hotline: 021-200 2700. Intercity: 021 643 2711.

MINWORTH USED to be the frontier between open country and the West Midlands conurbation, but the building of a high tech business park on the towpath side between Minworth Green and Wigginshill Road bridges has blurred the once distinct boundary. Corn fields remain defiantly agricultural on the opposite bank, but the more cynical may feel that it is only a matter of time before the prices for building land outweigh the marginal profits of the annual harvest; the new orbital toll road will cross the canal somewhere around here.

If, then, you want to avoid overnight mooring in a built-up area, you would be advised to tie up no further west than "The Kingsley" steak bar by Wigginshill Road Bridge. Not that the stretch of canal between Bromford and Minworth is uninteresting, reference to three 20th century maps revealed a cycle of change. An iron foundry was using the Tame for power as early as 1605, but neither the advent of the canal or the railway encouraged much industrial development. In 1916, however, the tyre makers Dunlop built a huge works on a 400 acre greenfield site which became known as Fort Dunlop. To transport the workforce to and from this new plant, Dunlop operated a small fleet of passenger carrying narrowboats between Aston and Bromford until the neighbouring Tyburn Road was laid with tram tracks. Apparently the 2½ mile, lock-free journey took around 35 minutes, and each boat could seat a hundred passengers. In 1938 the fields east of Fort Dunlop were occupied by one of the 'shadow' munitions factories as Britain armed for war. During the next seven years 11,564 Spitfires were built at the plant. The works was handily placed for test flights, for across the Chester Road stood Castle Bromwich aerodrome which had seen Birmingham's very first flying demonstration in 1911. After the war the aerodrome was run down and replaced, in the early Sixties, by the sprawling estate of Castle Vale: five thousand homes in blocks of flats rising to sixteen floors; and 'They' wonder why there are social problems!

In his book, "Number One", former canal boat captain, Tom Foxon, writes in detail of his experiences on the Birmingham & Fazeley in the mid 1950s. At that time substantial tonnages of coal were still being carried by canal from the collieries of North Warwickshire to the factory furnaces of Birmingham aboard 'Joey boats', boatman's parlance for narrow boats used for short-haul work and not designed for living aboard. The men who worked these largely horse-drawn boats knew this canal as 'The Old Cut' and in his book Tom describes the working practices of the era, commenting wryly that this was "the most depressing (route) experienced in his boating career." You'll just have to take it from us that matters have improved since those days – well relatively!

Summary of Facilities
Clusters of typical suburban shops line the A38 which parallels the canal, but access is not always convenient and mooring less than salubrious. MINWORTH has two food shops. There are lots of 'road-house' pubs, most of which have been enhanced into steak bars, the most convenient being THE KINGSLEY (so close to the canal that you could moor up to the beer pumps) by Wigginshill Road bridge. If you're in a real hurry, there's a KENTUCKY FRIED CHICKEN drive-in (for cars not boats) adjacent to Berwood Common bridge.

PASSING THROUGH the 57, towpath-equipped, yards of Curdworth Tunnel, the Birmingham & Fazeley spends five miles in the company of the county of Warwickshire, traversing a largely agricultural landscape interspersed with gravel pits. The M42 motorway runs parallel to the canal as it negotiates the Curdworth Locks, an excellently kept flight looked after with obvious passion by the lock-keeper at Dunton Wharf. The canal cottages along this length are numbered in the BCN sequence, a reminder that the B&F merged with the Birmingham Canal in 1794. Not far north from Dunton Wharf, along the A446 is the Belfry Hotel and its famous golf course. Another sporting association belongs to Bodymoor Heath, where Aston Villa have their football training ground. The bottom lock is overlooked by a quartet of canal cottages. Life must be pleasant here if, as one supposes, the inhabitants find the isolation conducive. Skeins of geese rise into the wide skies from flooded gravel workings; but for the noise of distant machinery, it could be some remote East Anglian marsh. But gravel has been extracted from the valley of the Tame since the 1930s; originally by dredger, later by dragline. Nowadays conveyor belts – like the one which crosses the canal by Fisher's Mill bridge – carry the minerals to screening and washing plants where they are sorted into varying types of aggregates. The bulk of it goes out by lorry, of course, but a trickle leaves by traditional narrowboat, making its way up to Rothern's yard at Atherstone on the Coventry Canal.

Curdworth

The village street is reached by crossing the busy A4097. Curdworth is one of several Warwickshire villages claiming to be at the centre of England. It is also reputed to be the oldest settlement in this part of the world and is named after Crida, not the cooker makers, but the first king of Mercia.

Eating & Drinking

WHITE HORSE – adjacent Curdworth Bridge. M&B, food, garden.
THE BEEHIVE – far end of village. Ansells 'all-day' pub.

Shopping

Post office stores & newspapers; open daily except for Tue & Sun afternoons.

Bodymoor Heath
Eating & Drinking

DOG & DOUBLET – canalside Cheatles Farm Bridge. M&B, bar & restaurant food. A rambling Georgian pub with attractive interiors and a garden with a dovecot. One of the best canal pubs in the Midlands.
MARSTON FARM HOTEL – adjacent canal near Marston Farm Bridge. Hotel offering bar or restaurant meals. Tel: Tamworth 872133 for bookings.

Places to Visit

KINGSBURY WATER PARK – Multi-recreation centre redeveloped from abandoned gravel workings. Adventure playground, boating & paddling pools, trim trail, picnic sites, nature trails with hides and interpretive centre with coffee shop. Tel: Tamworth 872660.

Minworth
23
Broad Balk Bridge
Curdworth Church Bridge
Curdworth Bridge
Curdworth Tunnel 52 metres
Coleshill South-West
Curdworth
Baylis's Bridge
Dunton Wharf
Curdworth Top Lock
Lichfield
M42
A4097
A446
Dunton Wharf Bridge
9
A446
Fox's Bridge
Willday's Farm Bridge
Marston Lane Bridge
White Bridge
N
Warwickshire
Curdworth Locks 76ft 4ins
Marston Field Bridge
Lee Marston
A4097
Bodymoor Heath
Double Bridge
Hotel
Cheatle's Farm Bridge
Bodymoor Heath Bridge
M42
gravel pits
Conveyor
2
Kingsbury Water Park
Curdworth Bottom Lock
gravel pits
River Tame
Visitor Centre i
Nottingham

SOUTH OF FAZELEY lies one of the 'little wonders' of the inland waterways, the exotic Drayton footbridge, where two Gothic towers encase spiral staircases and support an otherwise ordinary open iron span; a delightful functional folly: have your camera ready.

Fazeley Junction isn't anywhere near as pretty as Fradley, but it exudes a certain grubby grandeur, exemplified by the handsome junction house and the big mills which might have escaped from Oldham or Rochdale. The Birmingham & Fazeley Canal reached here in 1789 and the following year Sir Robert Peel, father of the Prime Minister, opened the first mill here for cotton spinning and calico printing. They were powered by the waters of the Bourne Brook which joins the Tame nearby. A second mill, of five

storeys, was built in 1883 for the weaving of haberdashery and upholstery. Both mills remain to entertain the industrial archaelogist.

British Waterways new regional headquarters overlook the canal at Peel's Wharf, along with adjoining housing, the sale of which presumably paid for the offices. More new housing is springing up on the opposite bank, but by Bonehill bridge the canal retreats into a small pool soothingly bordered by overhanging alders, a quiet haunt of fishermen and dragonflies on hot days. There are glimpses to the north of Tamworth Castle and the imposing parish church of St Editha, then the canal looses itself in and amongst the cabbage fields, which it is often called upon to irrigate, before reaching Hopwas.

Fazeley
Reminds you of one of those Mid West American towns where the shops and houses seem incidental to the interchange: more acres of ashphalt than anything else. Nevertheless, Fazeley is a useful port of call for canal travellers, and the locals are as friendly and helpful as the Watling Street's traffic is terrifying.

Eating & Drinking
THREE TUNS – canalside to west of junction; customer moorings and water point.
THREE HORSE SHOES – Lichfield Street. Village centre alternative; Draught Bass.
Fish & Chips.

Shopping
General stores, butchers, newsagents, post office and off licence. No banks. Cycle hire from Freestones on Watling Street.

Places to Visit
DRAYTON MANOR PARK – Open daily Easter to October, admission charge, access on A4091 adjacent to Drayton footbridge. Tel: Tamworth (0827) 287979. Leisure park with zoo, amusements, nature trail and woodland walks.

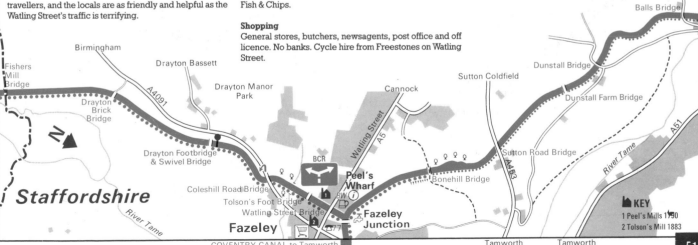

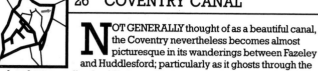

NOT GENERALLY thought of as a beautiful canal, the Coventry nevertheless becomes almost picturesque in its wanderings between Fazeley and Huddlesford; particularly as it ghosts through the brackeny woodlands of Hopwas, where red flags warn of military manoeuvres. Glibly we call this the Coventry Canal, but actually – and by now the presence of nameplates and not numbers on the bridges should have quickened your suspicions – the canal between Fazeley and Whittington was built by the Birmingham & Fazeley company. The Coventry Canal received its Act of Parliament in 1768, but seventeen years later it was nowhere near completion; primarily through a shortage of capital, but also, historians suspect, because some of the directors had interests in the Warwickshire coalfield and were worried by the thought that their through route, were it to be finished, would boost trade from the North Staffordshire pits at the expense of their own. In frustration the Trent & Mersey and Birmingham & Fazeley companies undertook to jointly build the canal between Fradley and Fazeley. The two met at Whittington in 1790, at a point recently graced with a plaque provided by the local branch of the I.W.A. commemorating the bicentenary of the joining. So pleasant scenery and canal history mingle as you negotiate the lower valley of the Tame; passing Fisherwick, where the houses face the canal in Dutch fashion, rather than turning their backs on it as is more usual in England; and arcing round Whittington, where you come upon the strange puzzle of 'Whittington Lock'. At Huddlesford a short arm – all that remains of the Wyrley & Essington Canal – is used for moorings by Lichfield Cruising Club who also occupy the attractive, lattice-windowed junction house pictured on the title page of this Companion.

Map labels

Lichfield
Dixon's Br.
Lichfield Road Bridge
Hopwas School Bridge
Hopwas
River Tame
A51
Tamworth
Hopwas Wood Bridge
Hopwas Woods
Tamhorn Park Bridge
Tamhorn House Bridge
Tamhorn Farm Bridge
Hademoor House Bridge
Hademoor Farm Bridge
Whittington Bridge
Whittington
Fisherwick
(Course of W & E Canal to Ogley Junction)
Lichfield Cruising Club
Huddlesford Junction
Lichfield
Stafford
25 · 78 · 79 · 80 · 81 · 82 · 83 · 2

Hopwas
The army's occupation of Hopwas Woods has preserved them from exploitation and they continue to contribute to the seductive setting of the village at the base of a hill beside the River Tame. A six arch stone bridge carries the busy road from Tamworth to Lichfield across the river, whilst the little church is of charming 'arts & crafts' style. There are two canalside pubs and a little post office stores.

Whittington
Explosions of new housing have turned the old village into just another Lichfield suburb, and there is little here to attract the passing boater other than a post office stores, Co-op, butcher and antiques shop. There are three pubs as well, THE SWAN by bridge 80 being nearest the canal. Buses run to Lichfield, a worthwhile excursion ashore perhaps?

Huddlesford
The few houses of Huddlesford *huddle* together in the shadow of the railway embankment. There are no shops, but THE PLOUGH is a nice enough pub with a canalside garden.

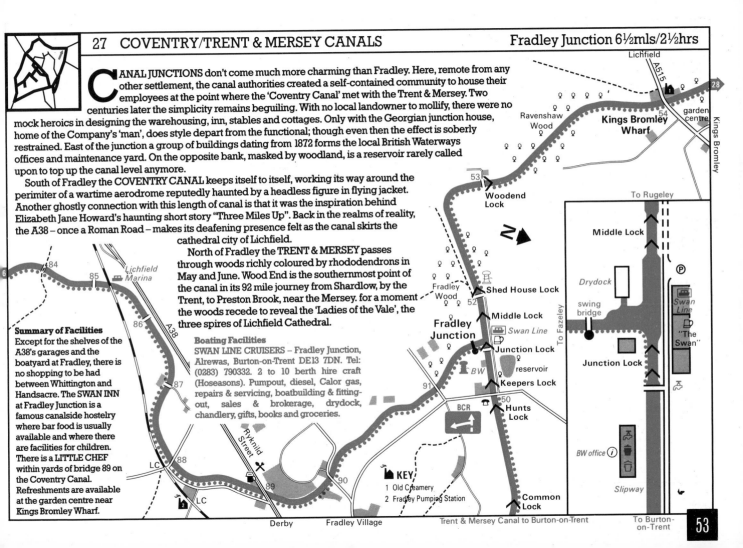

CANAL JUNCTIONS don't come much more charming than Fradley. Here, remote from any other settlement, the canal authorities created a self-contained community to house their employees at the point where the 'Coventry Canal' met with the Trent & Mersey. Two centuries later the simplicity remains beguiling. With no local landowner to mollify, there were no mock heroics in designing the warehousing, inn, stables and cottages. Only with the Georgian junction house, home of the Company's 'man', does style depart from the functional; though even then the effect is soberly restrained. East of the junction a group of buildings dating from 1872 forms the local British Waterways offices and maintenance yard. On the opposite bank, masked by woodland, is a reservoir rarely called upon to top up the canal level anymore.

South of Fradley the COVENTRY CANAL keeps itself to itself, working its way around the perimeter of a wartime aerodrome reputedly haunted by a headless figure in flying jacket. Another ghostly connection with this length of canal is that it was the inspiration behind Elizabeth Jane Howard's haunting short story "Three Miles Up". Back in the realms of reality, the A38 – once a Roman Road – makes its deafening presence felt as the canal skirts the cathedral city of Lichfield.

North of Fradley the TRENT & MERSEY passes through woods richly coloured by rhododendrons in May and June. Wood End is the southernmost point of the canal in its 92 mile journey from Shardlow, by the Trent, to Preston Brook, near the Mersey. for a moment the woods recede to reveal the 'Ladies of the Vale', the three spires of Lichfield Cathedral.

Summary of Facilities
Except for the shelves of the A38's garages and the boatyard at Fradley, there is no shopping to be had between Whittington and Handsacre. The SWAN INN at Fradley Junction is a famous canalside hostelry where bar food is usually available and where there are facilities for children. There is a LITTLE CHEF within yards of bridge 89 on the Coventry Canal. Refreshments are available at the garden centre near Kings Bromley Wharf.

Boating Facilities
SWAN LINE CRUISERS – Fradley Junction, Alrewas, Burton-on-Trent DE13 7DN. Tel: (0283) 790332. 2 to 10 berth hire craft (Hoseasons). Pumpout, diesel, Calor gas, repairs & servicing, boatbuilding & fitting-out, sales & brokerage, drydock, chandlery, gifts, books and groceries.

Lichfield
Kings Bromley
28
garden centre
54
Ravenshaw Wood
Kings Bromley Wharf
To Rugeley
53
Woodend Lock
Middle Lock
N
Drydock
6
84
85
Lichfield Marina
P
swing bridge
Swan Line
52
Fradley Wood
Shed House Lock
To Fazeley
86
A38
Middle Lock
"The Swan"
Fradley Junction
Swan Line
Junction Lock
87
Junction Lock
reservoir
BW
Keepers Lock
91
BW office
BCR
50
Hunts Lock
LC
88
Ryknild Street
Slipway
89
LC
90
KEY
1 Old Creamery
2 Fradley Pumping Station
Common Lock
To Burton-on-Trent

BETWEEN FRADLEY AND HANDSACRE the canal winds through a village-less tract of country, comprehensively agricultural now, but betraying signs of the wild heathland it must once have been, in its sandy soil, gorse, bracken and gnarled oak trees.

Armitage and Shanks are synonomous with toilet plumbing, their trade marks are emblazoned on public conveniences throughout the world. Once they were separate firms, they merged in 1969, but the site alongside the canal at ARMITAGE dates back to 1817. Sanitaryware became a speciality in the 19th century under the management of Edward Johns – the origin of the Americanism 'going to the John'. Today the factory is huge and convincingly prosperous, and Armitage Shanks are a public limited company with a seemingly 'watertight' future.

Connections are apparent with another famous earthenware firm at Spode House and Hawkesyard Priory. Josiah Spode, a member of the North Staffordshire pottery family, left this house to a Dominican Order in 1893 and the monks proceeded to build a priory in the grounds. The priory is now a nursing home, the original house faces the canal, its Gothic facade somewhat at odds with the power station opposite.

Passing beneath the A513 the canal narrows and negotiates a rocky cutting. One-way working is the order of the day. This was formerly the site of Armitage Tunnel, a dramatic unlined bore through the rock face. The canal hereabouts is concrete lined. It has suffered considerably from subsidence caused by mining. Just how far the bed of the canal has dropped can be judged by the base of bridge 60.

The ranks of canalside collieries are steadily diminishing. Closure of Lea Hall Colliery was announced at the end of 1990. The pit had only opened thirty years before, a then modern showcase for the NCB. Much of its ouput went directly to Rugeley power station, but in announcing its closure, British Coal claimed that a series of unforseen geological faults had turned the mine into the most costly in Britain.

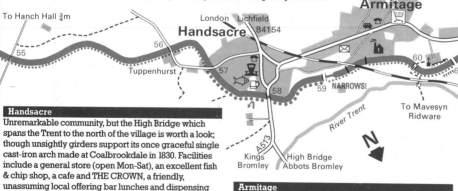

isn't easy on what is a rather narrow and tortuous section of canal.

Handsacre

Unremarkable community, but the High Bridge which spans the Trent to the north of the village is worth a look; though unsightly girders support its once graceful single cast-iron arch made at Coalbrookdale in 1830. Facilities include a general store (open Mon-Sat), an excellent fish & chip shop, a cafe and THE CROWN, a friendly, unassuming local offering bar lunches and dispensing particularly well kept Draught Bass. Two places to visit if you have the benefit of bicycles are: HANCH HALL, 1 mile west of bridge 55, Tel: 0543 490308 for opening times; and RIDWARE ARTS CENTRE 3 miles north of bridge 58, ask locally for directions.

Armitage

Guidebooks point to the 'interesting' church above the canal by bridge 61, but it is the Armitage Shanks works which dominates. A path leads across the river to the splendidly isolated village of Mavesyn Ridware. There is a good choice of shops on the main road, but mooring

Eating & Drinking

THE PLUM PUDDING – canalside pub (bridge 61a) which has dropped considerably below the level of the cut because of the subsidence. Ansells, bar and restaurant meals, patio.

OLD FARMHOUSE RESTAURANT – across the road from the "Plum Pudding". A smart and locally renowned restaurant. Not for those with an eye on their bank balance. Tel: Armitage 490353.

ASH TREE INN – canalside bridge 62. Refurbished Banks's pub offering a variety of food.

THE RIVER'S SLOW influence pervades the canal, and the pair wander across the landscape like indolent lovers on a long afternoon, chaperoned at a discreet distance by the recumbent mass of The Chase.

RUGELEY was infamous for its smelly canalside tannery, but all trace of this has vanished beneath housing. Now it is the cooling towers of the power stations which dominate; Rugeley 'A' was opened in 1963, Rugeley 'B' nine years later. Both are coal fired, between them they use up to 15,000 tonnes of coal a day. The older station has an output of 600 megawatts, the newer 1,000.

At Brindley Bank the canal suddenly stops running parallel with the Trent and turns sharply to cross it, as though Brindley had been screwing up his courage to bridge the river. Several big houses were built by prosperous landowners in this enchanting countryside. The stuccoed facade of Bishton Hall overlooks the canal. Nowadays it is a preparatory school with a cricket ground shaded by ancient chestnut trees bordering the water. Another mansion, Wolseley Hall, stood opposite on the far bank of the river. It was demolished long ago, but the grounds have been restored as ornamental gardens. Wolseley Bridge has gracefully spanned the Trent here since 1800. It was designed by John Rennie, best known in the canal world for his work on the Kennet & Avon Canal.

West of bridge 68 the towpath forms the route of the 'Staffordshire Way'.

KEY
1 Rugeley A & B Power Stations
2 Brindley Bank Pumping Station
3 Site of tannery
4 Former mill

Rugeley
For the first time in three hundred years Rugeley finds itself without a coal mine on its doorstep. A thousand jobs were lost when Lea Hall pit closed, but this is a resilient little town well versed in the vicissitudes of existence. Life here is lived on the cheap but with a certain deadpan dignity. A consoling beauty is to be found up on The Chase, here in the tight-knit streets and on the old coal board estates is thrift and graft and a perverse civic pride. Old King Coal is dead, long live the king.

Eating & Drinking
GEORGE & BERTIES – Albion Street. An unusual cafe with a central bar around which customers sit perched on high stools continental fashion.
LA TERRAZZA – Albion Street. Italian restaurant.
ARIA – Anson Street. Take-away kebabs etc.

Shopping
Moor north of bridge 66 for easiest access to nearby town centre. Branches of most banks, market on Tue, Thur-Sat, supermarket very close to canal. Lots of good cake shops!

Public Transport
BUSES – services throughout the Trent Valley and Cannock Chase. If you have half a day to spare take the Green Bus to Cannock, a magical excursion up and over The Chase. Tel: Stafford (0785) 223344 for details of all services.

TRAINS – sparse weekday service along the Trent Valley. Tel: (0782) 411411.

Wolseley & Colwich
Two little communities strung out along the A51. Wolseley has a craft centre, antiques showroom, art gallery and garden park; all accessible from bridge 70. THE WOLSELEY ARMS (1) does bar meals Mon-Sun lunchtimes and Tue-Sat nights, the restaurant is open Tue-Sun. It is an attractive pub, long ago used by the promoters of the canal for meetings. There are two stores in Colwich, best reached from the lock via the footpath past the church. Buses run from here to Stafford.

THE TRENT & MERSEY and Staffordshire & Worcestershire canals meet at Great Haywood, as do the rivers Sow and Trent. Brindley always found it easier to follow river valleys, and this must have been an obvious choice for a canal junction in establishing his plan for a 'Grand Cross' of man made waterways linking the four great English estuaries: Humber, Thames, Severn and Mersey. With the completion of the Staffs & Worcs in 1772, and the Trent & Mersey five years later, Haywood became a canal junction of major importance, as significant to transport in the 18th century as any motorway interchange today. One can only marvel at the simplicity of it all – two quiet ribbons of water meeting beneath a bridge of exquisite beauty – and compare it sadly with transport interchanges of the 20th century, acres of concrete, noise and pollution. Where did we go wrong?

There is little chance of a wrong turning on the canal at Great Haywood. A prominent finger post directs travellers concisely enough to Wolverhampton, The Trent or The Potteries. Between here and Colwich the TRENT & MERSEY is at its most memorably beautiful as it skirts the boundary of Shugborough. On one bank beechwoods tumble down to the water's edge. On the other, across the Trent, there are glimpses of the curious statues, antiquities and follies which pepper the grounds of this famous home of the Anson family. Two railway lines converge at Colwich, the scene of a terrifying collision in 1986 between two Inter-city expresses. One of the drivers died but over seven hundred passengers walked away from the wreckage virtually unscathed. A little memorial garden has been planted beside the track to commemorate the driver. Colwich Lock lies in an attractive setting between the village church, a picturesque farm and a bend in the river. From bridge 72 you can take an idyllic walk to Seven Springs and on up into The Chase itself.

Through the arch of bridge 109 – an 18th century fusion of functional engineering and enduring loveliness – the STAFFORDSHIRE & WORCESTERSHIRE CANAL can be seen heading westwards on its 46 mile journey down to the Severn at Stourport. Two aqueducts carry it across the Trent and a millstream. A couple of miles further on it crosses the Sow. Between these river crossings, though, the canal suddenly, outrageously, casts off its inhibitions and widens into a broad lake of quite un-canal-like proportions, bordered by thick reedbeds inhabited by a gorgeous array of wildfowl. Boaters will find their craft looping the loop out of sheer exuberance. This is Tixall Wide or Broadwater and there are two theories for its surprising existence. Some maintain that the canal was widened into an artificial lake to placate the owner of Tixall Hall, others that the expanse of water predates the canal, that it was naturally formed, and that Izaak Walton learnt to fish here. Accept whichever explanation suits you, but don't miss the extraordinary Elizabethan gatehouse of Tixall which overlooks the Wide. The hall itself, where Mary Queen of Scots was imprisoned for a fortnight in 1586, was demolished long ago. The gatehouse, though, belongs to the admirable Landmark Trust who specialise in the holiday letting of unusual and historic properties such as this.

The Haywoods

The villages of Great and Little Haywood are separated by the long, high brick wall of the Shugborough estate. Dormitory housing has inevitably expanded both populations, but the centres remain peaceful and unspoilt; especially so in the charming lane leading from Great Haywood, under the railway and over the canal to the Essex Bridge, one of the finest examples of a packhorse bridge imaginable. On hot summer days the locals splash about in the water here as their forebears must have done for generations.

Eating & Drinking

CLIFFORD ARMS – (1) Gt. Haywood. Bass, bar meals, garden.
LOCK HOUSE – adjacent Haywood Lock. Tea rooms and licenced restaurant.
RED LION – (2) Little Haywood. Ind Coope, bar food.

Shopping

Little Haywood has a post office stores (open daily inc Sun am) and newsagent. Great Haywood has two small supermarkets, a post office, and a farm shop alongside the junction. West of the junction roving bridge the former toll house is an outlet for canalware and crafts.

Places to Visit

SHUGBOROUGH – access via Haywood Lock and Essex Bridge. Open daily April to December. Admission charge. Attractions include mansion, county museum, working farm, gardens, National Trust shop and cafeteria. A visit to the farm is particularly enjoyable for children. Frequent special events and a regular point of departure for hot air balloons.

Public Transport

BUSES – regular Midland Red service through *Little* Haywood to Stafford. Tel: Stafford (0785) 223344.

Boatyard & Hire Base

ANGLO WELSH – Head office: Canal Basin, Leicester Road, Market Harborough LE16 7BJ. Tel: MH (0858) 466910. Boatyard tel: Little Haywood 881711. 2 to 10 berth hire craft. Pumpout, diesel, gas, repairs & servicing, guidebooks & toilets.

Milford

A motorist's gateway to Shugborough and The Chase unlikely to hold much attraction for canal travellers. Facilities, however, include a steak bar, fast food outlet, post office store, newsagent and farm shop. Access from either bridge 105 or 106.

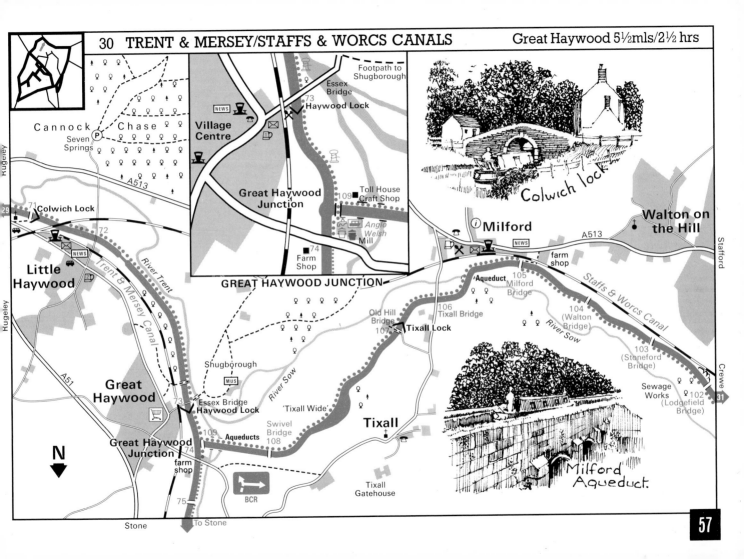

Footpath to Shugborough

Essex Bridge

Haywood Lock 73

NEWS

Cannock Chase

Seven Springs P

A513

Village Centre

Great Haywood Junction

Toll House Craft Shop 109

Anglo Welsh Mill

74 Farm Shop

Colwich lock

Milford i

Walton on the Hill

A513

71 **Colwich Lock**

29

72

NEWS

Little Haywood

Trent & Mersey Canal

River Trent

GREAT HAYWOOD JUNCTION

farm shop

Aqueduct 105 Milford Bridge

Staffs & Worcs Canal

104 (Walton Bridge)

River Sow

103 (Stoneford Bridge)

Sewage Works

102 (Lodgefield Bridge)

31

Crewe

Stafford

Rugeley

106 Tixall Bridge

Old Hill Bridge

107 **Tixall Lock**

Shugborough MUS

Great Haywood

A51

73

Essex Bridge **Haywood Lock**

River Sow

'Tixall Wide'

Swivel Bridge 108

Tixall

109 Aqueducts

Great Haywood Junction

74 farm shop

75

BCR

To Stone

Tixall Gatehouse

Milford Aqueduct.

N

Stone

57

THE CANAL slips largely unmolested through the eastern outskirts of Stafford. So self-effacing are the suburbs that herons are often to be encountered, fishing their beats until disturbed by your approach, at which they flap ponderously away across the gardens and fields to rejoin the canal ahead of you.

The county town stood an aloof mile to the west of the Staffs & Worcs which, in true Brindley fashion, followed the easy contours of the Penk valley. Plans to construct a branch were dropped in favour of a simple lock down into the Sow, the river being dredged and realigned to take boats as far as a terminal basin at Green Bridge in the centre of Stafford. The navigation was opened in 1816 and used until the end of the Great War. Those with a passion for the past can walk along the riverbank to the town centre, imagining as they go, the slow progress of a narrowboat up the winding Sow. Stafford Boat Club, with their substantial and impressive club house, occupy a former brickworks arm near Hazelstrine Bridge.

The inherent other-worldliness of the canal undergoes strange fluctuations in fortune hereabouts. Nowhere could be more apparently remote than Deptmore Lock, with its towering lockside conifers: the reclusive occupant of the old lock-keeper's cottage commutes to the outside world by dinghy. Acton Trussell, though, which you expect with such a name to be an exquisite, picture-book English village, disappoints with its postured architectural formality, fully deserving the motorway on its doorstep. Wildwood conjures up images of friendly, furry little creatures out of "The Wind in the Willows", but in reality it is a housing estate on a hill.

Stafford

One of England's lesser-known county towns, Stafford has always been too self-effacing for its own good; but there are signs now that it has woken to its tourist potential. The town centre is over a mile from the canal at Radford Bridge, and there will be many boaters who consider that just too far to make the effort, but there are frequent buses and those with a little time at their disposal will find a visit to Stafford entertaining. Your first stop should be the Ancient High House in Greengate Street - the main thoroughfare - which houses the tourist information centre. Dating from 1595, it's thought to be the largest timber-framed town house remaining in England. Inside there's a heritage exhibition tracing Stafford's history since 913 AD when Ethelfleda, daughter of Alfred the Great, fortified the settlement against marauding Danish invaders. King Charles I stayed at the High House in 1642 and in later years Izaak Walton visited with relatives who owned it. A 'town trail' leaflet is available to guide you around the best of Stafford's surprisingly rich roll-call of historic buildings.

Eating & Drinking
There's no shortage of pubs and restaurants, but our own favourite is the SOUP KITCHEN in Church Lane, a quaint and bustling eatery open for coffees, lunches and teas Mon-Sat (EC Wed). If you haven't time to reach the town centre the TRUMPET INN steak bar is canalside at bridge 98.

Shopping
All services, markets on Tue, Fri & Sat. Good shopping centre featuring all the well known 'high street' names plus many attractive individual shops tucked away down some of the twisting side streets. The Art Gallery houses a craft shop (open Tue-Sat) specialising in contemporary works of high standard.

Places to Visit
TOURIST INFORMATION CENTRE - Ancient High House, Greengate St. Tel: Stafford (0785) 40204.
STAFFORD CASTLE - 1ml west of centre on A518. Waymarked trail around Norman motte & bailey remains.

Public Transport
BUSES - Midland Red and Potteries Motor Traction services to all parts of Midlands. Tel: Stafford (0785) 42997.
TRAINS - Major railhead. Tel: Stafford 211377.

LOCKS COME THICK and fast as the canal ascends to, or descends from, its summit level. The motorway retreats, only to be replaced by the housing estates which cling-wrap the otherwise agreeable little town of Penkridge. Yet a mile on either side the countryside is characterised by rolling farmland lifting to the bulwark of Cannock Chase.

The towpath between bridges 90 and 96 is borrowed by the "Staffordshire Way". Bridge 89 was nicknamed 'Fancy Bridge' because of its rather ostentatious style. It led to Teddesley Hall, a big mansion demolished in the 1950s following its use as a prison camp for German officers. Sadly, the once ornate balustrades of the bridge have been infilled by brickwork.

A single line railway crosses the canal, passes beneath the M6 and heads off to Littleton Colliery at the foot of The Chase. Once the canal shared in this traffic and there was an extensive basin where coal was loaded from a central pier by gravity on to day boats bound for the Black Country. In the days before nationalisation of the coal industry Littleton mine had a poor safety record and was known locally as 'Slaughter Pit'.

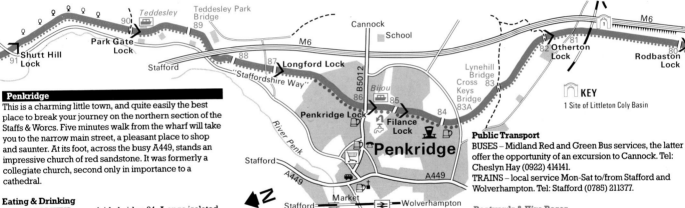

Penkridge

This is a charming little town, and quite easily the best place to break your journey on the northern section of the Staffs & Worcs. Five minutes walk from the wharf will take you to the narrow main street, a pleasant place to shop and saunter. At its foot, across the busy A449, stands an impressive church of red sandstone. It was formerly a collegiate church, second only in importance to a cathedral.

Eating & Drinking

THE CROSS KEYS – canalside bridge 84. A once isolated pub described by Rolt in "Narrow Boat". Now surrounded by houses but still popular with boaters. Draught Bass and Springfield Mild, bar food ex Sun night.

THE BOAT – canalside bridge 96. Attractively refurbished pub overlooking the wharf and Penkridge Lock. Good choice of home-cooking.

THE MOAT HOUSE – canalside bridge 92 (Acton Trussell). Restaurant and bars in former moated farmhouse. Offside mooring for patrons.

There are two fish and chip shops and several other pubs.

Shopping

Some lovely little shops of individual character in the main street, and if you really need it, a supermarket as well. Lloyds and Barclays banks on the A449. Thriving and atmospheric market on Wednesdays and Saturdays beside the river.

KEY

1 Site of Littleton Coly Basin

Public Transport

BUSES – Midland Red and Green Bus services, the latter offer the opportunity of an excursion to Cannock. Tel: Cheslyn Hay (0922) 414141.

TRAINS – local service Mon-Sat to/from Stafford and Wolverhampton. Tel: Stafford (0785) 211377.

Boatyards & Hire Bases

TEDDESLEY – Teddesley Road, Penkridge, Stafford ST19 5RH. Tel: Stafford (0785) 714692. 2 to 8 berth hire craft. Pumpout, diesel, Shell gas, repairs & servicing, boatbuilding & fitting out, crane, chandlery and, guidebooks.

BIJOU LINE – The Wharf, Penkridge, Staffs. ST19 5DK. Tel: Stafford (0785) 712732. 2 to 12 berth hire craft (Hoseasons). Pumpout, diesel, Elsan & refuse disposal gas, repairs & servicing.

MIDLAND CHANDLERS – located at Teddesley. Tel: Stafford 712437.

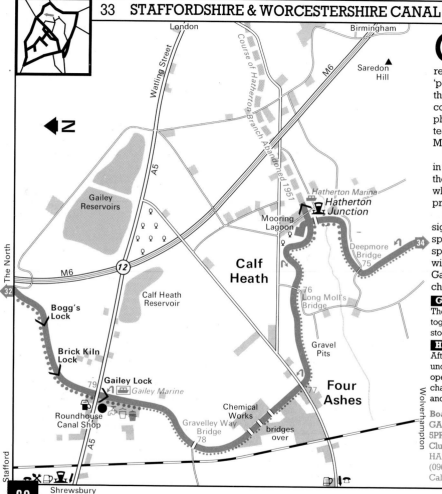

CALF HEATH is a strangely isolated tract of country, pancake flat, and crossed by a grid of sullen little roads, with here and there a huddle of houses, gathered reassuringly together like something out of Van Gogh's early 'potato field' paintings. The canal all but boxes the compass of this gravel pit riddled landscape, so that the Chase with its communications tower and the chemical works with its phalanx of flaring chimneys, appear to move about you, teasing you into geographic insecurity, like a game of Blind Man's Buff.

The last load of Cannock coal came off the Hatherton Branch in 1949 and it was abandoned a couple of years later. However, the illusion of a junction remains, because the bottom lock (of what was once a flight of eight in three miles) is still used to provide access to moorings.

Watling Street crosses the canal at Gailey. The most significant feature here is the 'round house' which is now a splendid canal shop. There is something extraordinarily spellbinding about cylindrical buildings – Martello towers, windmills and lighthouses; even the Bull Ring Rotunda! and Gailey round house, in its lock-side setting, has a particular charm which you will want to try and capture on film.

Gailey

The Canal Shop stocks an excellent range of gifts, books and maps together with a modest, but useful, selection of groceries; and they also stock Sunday papers.

Hatherton

After a period of closure, the shop by Hatherton Junction has re-opened under the auspices of 'Hatherton Marina'. The post office counter is only open on Thursdays, but there's a good range of groceries and some chandlery and giftware too. They do teas by the rosebeds in Summer and there's a licenced restaurant too.

Boatyards & Hirebase

GAILEY MARINE - The Wharf, Watling Street, Gailey, Stafford ST19 5PR. Tel: Standeford (0902) 790612. 2 to 8 berth hire craft (Blue Riband Club). Pumpout, Calor gas, repairs & servicing, boatbuilding.
HATHERTON MARINA – Kings Road, Calf Heath, Wolverhampton. Tel: (0902) 791622. Moorings, slipway, drydock, lift-out, boaters club house, Calor gas and diesel.

THE CANAL exchanges the lonely landscapes of Calf and Coven heaths for the industrial and suburban outskirts of Wolverhampton; the M54 motorway to Telford forming an obvious, though not intentional boundary. At Cross Green a former canal pub called "The Anchor" has become a popular steak bar and many boaters choose to moor here overnight.

As it passes beneath the M54 the canal crosses the county boundary between Staffordshire and the West Midlands, one of the new counties which had its origins in the local government changes of 1974. Many people still mourn the old county boundaries. It must have been galling, for instance, to have lived in Lincolnshire all one's life and wake up one morning in South Humberside. Similarly, as names go, Avon is no substitute for Somerset. West Midlands was possibly the dullest of all the new names,

and sounds as though it must have been the compromise of a committee. Black Country would have been a far more appropriate and resonant title. You can imagine its inhabitants enjoying a perverse pride in such a name. No-one could possibly show a flicker of interest in anyone who admitted to coming from the West Midlands.

The most significant canal feature of this length is 'Pendeford Rockin', the old boatmen's name for a shallow, but tellingly narrow cutting hewn by Brindley's navvies through a solid belt of sandstone which breaks through the clay strata at this point. The cutting, half a mile or so long, restricts the channel to such a degree that you begin to wonder if you have lost concentration and taken a wrong turn. There are, however, one or two passing places – as on a single lane road – where oncoming boats can be successfully negotiated without losing one's temper. Similar narrows occur on the Shropshire Union north of Autherley as that canal encounters the same difficult rock.

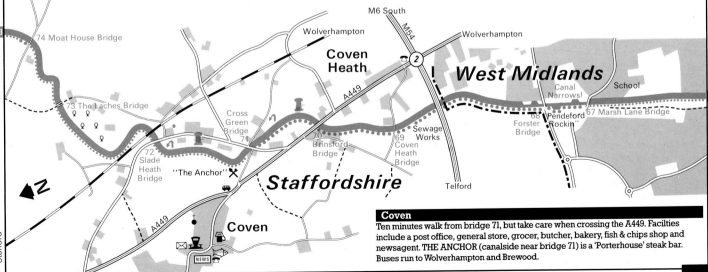

Coven

Ten minutes walk from bridge 71, but take care when crossing the A449. Facilties include a post office, general store, grocer, butcher, bakery, fish & chips shop and newsagent. THE ANCHOR (canalside near bridge 71) is a 'Porterhouse' steak bar. Buses run to Wolverhampton and Brewood.

Information

How to use the maps

There are thirty-four numbered maps. Their layout is indicated by the Route Planner on the inside of the front cover. Maps 1,2, 6-21 show the route of the STOURPORT RING; maps 9-12 & 22-34 the route of the BLACK COUNTRY RING; and maps 3 & 4 the connecting DUDLEY & STOURBRIDGE CANALS. The maps are easily read in either direction, a numbered arrow at the edge of each map indicating clearly the following map to which you should refer. A 'thumbnail' map at the top left hand corner of each map is a further indication of your overall position with regard to the canals of the West Midlands. Figures quoted at the top of each map refer to the distance and average cruising time for that particular page. An alternative indication of times can be found on the Route Planner.

Using the text

Each map is accompanied by a route commentary describing the landscape and placing the canal in its historic context. A brief sketch of towns and villages passed through is given, together with itemised details or summarised information on facilities likely to be of interest to canal users.

Eating & Drinking

Pubs, restaurants, cafes and fast food outlets considered to be of interest to canal users are mentioned. In the case of some pubs we quote an identification number within the tankard symbol to aid location. We don't set out to make judgements in an Egon Ronay sense, but, generally speaking, the more detail we give, the higher in esteem a particular establishment is likely to be. By the very nature of their trade, pubs and restaurants tend to change hands, alter their services, or simply close down, and we apologise in advance for any misleading entries in the text.

Shopping

Shopping in unfamiliar towns and villages is one of the unsung pleasures of canal travel. Our shopping details try to reflect the range of facilities available, from village stores to specialist retailers in city locations.

Places to Visit

Details are given in this category of Tourist Information Centres, museums and visitor centres etc within easy reach of the canal.

Public Transport

Information in this category is quoted particularly for the benefit of walkers who wish to walk 'one-way', using a bus or train in the opposite direction. Boaters, however, may find them of use when planning an excursion 'ashore'. Do, however, take the trouble to use the telephone number provided, bus services in particular are liable to alteration.

Boating Facilities

Every boatyard and hire base is marked on the relevant map and listed appropriately. It is not politic, nor practical for us to quote any indication of quality and cost applicable to hire fleets. We strongly recommend prospective hirers to obtain a relevant selection of brochures from bases of potential interest before making a firm booking.

Walking & Cycling

Towpaths are by and large the property of British Waterways and, though not always specifically 'rights of way', are open to the general public, no licence or permit being required for use by pedestrians. However, apart from the route of the BCN 'New Main Line' between Wolverhampton and Birmingham which is classified as a 'cycleway', cyclists must obtain a licence to ride towpaths in the region for an annual fee (1991 price) of £3.

The upkeep of towing paths is a costly exercise and one which British Waterways' budget does not always run too. In a growing number of instances, local authorities have become involved in towpath maintenance, to the benefit of all. To give you some idea of the state of any given length of towpath, we classify its condition into three categories on our maps. 'Good' can usually be taken to indicate the existence of a firm, wide and dry base, comfortable for both walking and cycling; 'adequate' hints at the chance of mud and excess vegetation, but can usually be considered passable; whilst 'poor' reflects conditions not conducive with enjoyable walking – a challenge for determined die-hards, but not much fun for a family stroll.

Boating

Boating on inland waterways is an established, though relatively small facet of the UK holiday industry. There are over 20,000 privately owned boats registered on the canals. In addition to this numerous firms offer boats for hire. These companies range from small operators with half a dozen boats to sizeable fleets run by companies with several bases.

Most hire craft have all the creature comforts you are likely to expect. In the excitement of planning a boating holiday you may give scant thought to the contents of your hire boat, but at the end of a hard day's boating such things take on more significance. A well equipped and reliable boat can make the difference between a good trip and a bad one.

Traditionally hire boats are booked out by the week or fortnight, though many firms now offer more flexible short breaks or extended weeks. All reputable hire firms give newcomers tuition in boat handling and lock working, and first-timers should soon find themselves adapting to the pace of things 'on the cut'.

Canal boating holidays are enjoyed by many thousands of people every year. As a holiday activity it can become compulsive. Many holiday firms find their customers coming back year after year, only losing them when they eventually succumb to the lure of a boat of their own!

Navigational Advice

Locks

Locks are part of the charm of canal cruising, but they are potentially dangerous environments for children, pets and careless adults. Use of them should be methodical and unhurried, whilst special care should be exercised in rain, frost and snow when slippery hazards abound. Apart from the basin locks at Diglis, Worcester and the automated locks on the River Severn between Worcester and Stourport, all the locks on the canals covered by this guide are of the familiar narrow-beam variety. all gates should be closed on leaving each chamber (unless courteously leaving them open for an approaching boat) and all paddles wound down.

The River Severn locks at Bevere, Holt and Lincomb are mechanised and manned. One prolonged blast on the boat horn should be enough to alert the keeper that you wish to use the lock. Be guided by the colour light signals, but wait for the signal to turn green and the gates to open before approaching too closely. The chambers of these locks are large and you may be sharing with other craft. Steading straps and chains are attached to chamber walls and these can be hand held to control the boat if there is any turbulence. Always follow the lock-keeper's advice, he will be in his control cabin as you pass through the lock. The navigation and weir channels leading to and from these locks are shown as enlargments on the relevant maps.

The basin locks at Worcester and Stourport are only open during timetabled hours, as are the river locks mentioned above, which usually close for a half-hour meal break at 1 and 5pm. Hire craft are likely to have up to date details on board, but private owners may acquire copies of "Cruising the Gloucester & Sharpness Canal & River Severn" from: British Waterways, Llanthony Warehouse, Gloucester GL1 2EH. Tel: Gloucester (0452) 25524.

Moorings

Mooring on the canals featured in this guide is per usual practice – ie on the towpath side, away from sharp bends, bridge-holes and narrows. Recommended moorings, of particular relevance to urban areas, are marked on the maps with an open bollard symbol. On the River Severn overnight moorings are available at Holt Lock and, at the discretion of the lock-keeper, at Bevere Lock. Several waterside pubs provide limited moorings for patrons. Remember always to turn upstream when coming in to moor on a river. In summer moorings on the Severn are at a premium and tend to be 'snapped-up' by late afternoon, a factor worth bearing in mind so as to avoid being stranded when the locks close for the night at around 7pm.

Floods

The river Severn is liable to flood at any time of the year at short notice. British Waterways staff will be on hand to help and advise at such times. If you are already on the river you must tie up at the nearest official moorings and remain there until further notice. At times of flood you may be denied access on to the river. Boat hire companies are used to the Severn's moods and will be sympathetic to genuine delays. If you have any enquiries regarding flood levels contact BW on Stourport (02993) 77662 or Worcester (0905) 356264.

Speed

A speed limit of 4mph exists throughout the canal system. On the River Severn the limits are 6mph upstream and 8mph downstream. However, as boats are not equipped with speedometers these limits tend to be widely interpreted. A square-bottomed boat travelling at 4mph along a shallow canal will create waves which cause damage to the banks. In effect there is only one firm rule which should govern speed, and that is that you should not be causing a wash or wave.

Closures

Closures – known as 'stoppages' on the canals – usually occur between November and April when maintenance work is undertaken. Occasionally, however, an emergency stoppage may be imposed at short notice, closing part of the route you intend to cruise. Up to date details are usually available from hire bases. Alternatively, British Waterways operate a recorded message service for private boaters detailing emergency stoppages. The number to ring is 071-723 8487.

Societies

The Inland Waterways Association was founded in 1946 to campaign for retention of the canal system. Many of the routes open to pleasure boaters now might not have been available but for this organisation. Several of the individual canals featured in this guide have their own support groups as well. Details of these and more information on the IWA itself can be obtained from: Inland Waterways Association, 114 Regent's Park Road, London NW1 8UQ. Tel: 071-586 2556.

Useful Contacts

Waterway Managers are responsible for individual sections of canal. They welcome enquiries from the general public, either in person or by telephone. The offices relevant to the canals covered by this guide are as follows:

Staffordshire & Worcestershire Canal
Stourport – Gailey
Norbury Junction
Staffs ST20 0PN
Tel: Stafford (0785) 284253
Gailey – Gt Haywood
Fradley Junction
Staffs DE13 7DN
Tel: Burton-on-Trent (0283) 790236

Trent & Mersey Canal
as Fradley above

Birmingham & Fazeley Canal
Fradley – Curdworth
Hartshill
Warks CV10 0TB
Tel: Nuneaton (0203) 392250

Birmingham Canal Navigations
Bradley
West Mids WV14 8DW
Tel: Wolverhampton (0902) 409010

Worcester & Birmingham Canal
Tardebigge
Worcs B60 1NF
Tel: Bromsgrove (0527) 72572

River Severn
Gloucester
Glos. GL1 2EH
Tel: Glos. (0452) 25524

Acknowledgements

CC users, Robert Foxon, Max Harper, A. Johnson, John Muskett and G.J. Wake took the trouble to write in with suggested amendments to the previous edtion and we are very grateful for their help and advice. The cover was designed by Brian Collings in an echo of Midland & Coast livery. Eric Leslie did all the internal illustration in his inimitable manner; the frontispiece is of Huddlesford Junction. Malcolm Barnes achieved the difficult task of improving on the previous edition's cartography; Characters did the 'origination' and Penwell the printing in their usual thorough manner and we would like to thank everyone involved for their contribution.